PLAY CONFIDENTLY

QUIET YOUR INNER CRITIC

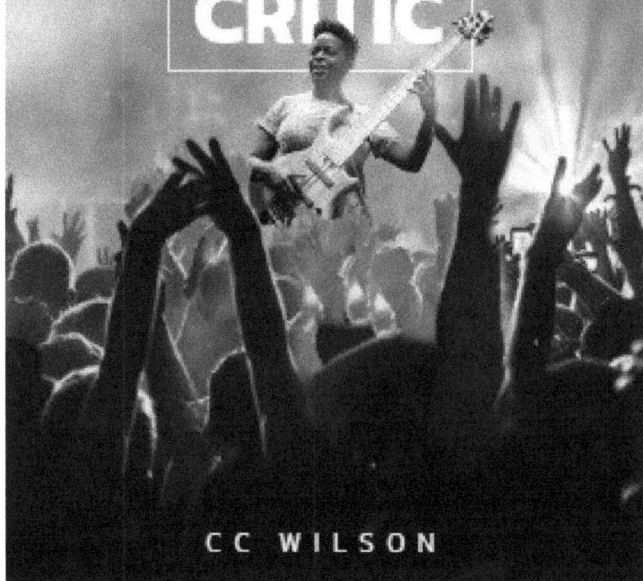

CC WILSON

Play Confidently: Quiet Your Inner Critic
Written by Sheryl "CC" Wilson

Copyright 2019 by Sheryl Wilson

Published 2019
Printed in the United States of America

ISBN Print Edition: 978-0-578-42907-6

Contents

ABOUT THE AUTHOR

CC, whose real is name Sheryl Wilson, is a professional bassist who inspires other musicians to improve their playing confidence. Like many musicians, CC's journey began as a childhood dream of becoming a rock star, 'playing' John Mellencamp songs on a tennis racquet 'guitar.' Inspired by the complex bass lines in songs by Iron Maiden and Rush, CC began learning to play the bass guitar at the age of 12. From learning heavy metal songs by ear to playing fun gigs with teen bands, CC's life revolved around music.

CC went on to play bass in the U.S. Navy Band San Diego and has over 12 years of professional experience performing Jazz, Top 40 Pop, and Latin music. She is a highly sought-after musician in the Washington, D.C. metro area, where she currently resides.

CC treats music as a language, and performing as a stimulating conversation between the band members and audience. She enjoys playing with different musicians and speaking with them on effective ways to build confidence in their performance.

PREFACE

Musicians want to share the joy of music by performing publicly, yet many suffer from performance anxiety. For many, this is a gap they can't close, leaving them with shaken confidence. The fear of failure, humiliation, and the unknown keeps them from reaching their potential.

Our inner critic wears us down with doubts about our abilities and our potential. People may tell us to simply relax and have fun. But, without the self-mastery to manage our emotions, we are unable to do that. Or, they may tell us to practice more. And while practice might give us some confidence, it doesn't necessarily give us the mental skills to be a great performer. So, what can we do?

Play Confidently: Quiet Your Inner Critic offers practical strategies for building performance confidence. Music students and seasoned performers alike will enjoy this inspiring book that takes a holistic approach to building confidence as a performer. It utilizes various techniques to help anyone have a better performance experience. It will help musicians of any ability or style, from new musicians who are afraid to play publicly to seasoned performers who are struggling with burnout.

At the end of most chapters, there are "Tune Ups" to help make the lessons practical in your daily life. Tune Ups are calls to actions designed to help you explore the barriers holding you back. Through increased self-awareness and peeling back the layers of your anxieties, you can, at the very least, manage your performance anxiety and find success.

I lay out the challenges every musician faces by sharing my own stories, experiences, and lessons. I'm no stranger to performance anxiety. There was a time when I gave up music completely because of my unshakeable self-doubt. This book is the story of how anxiety shaped my musical career, caused me to quit, and how I learned to manage it and become a highly sought-after performer.

Music vendors offer a plethora of technical instructional books, but there aren't many books that address performance improvement on an emotional or psychological level. Performance anxiety is such a common struggle, yet it's not talked about much. That's why I was inspired to write this book. It explores the journey that many musicians experience: they are born with confidence, but this slowly fades because of their own inner critic and they eventually reach a tipping point in their musical journey when they either master their anxiety or fail to reach their potential.

My goal is to help you reach your potential. In this book, you'll learn how to:

- control your performance nerves,
- master your talent,
- overcome your negative self-talk,
- stop comparing yourself to other musicians,
- book better gigs, and
- create a genuine connection with your audience.

I hope this book becomes a useful tool as you chase your musical dreams. Let's jump in!

- CC Wilson

INTRODUCTION

It was a fall night in 1999, and a local Los Angeles restaurant was hosting an open jazz jam. As a 22-year-old professional bassist, I was eager to make my mark on the L.A. music scene. Every musician knows that when it comes to performing, no one cares how much education you've had. It's whether or not you can play. And the best way to get your name out there is to hit the open jams and have people hear you perform.

I arrived at the restaurant to find a good band playing. Immediately, I felt that feeling I get every time I hear talented musicians and have to play with them. My palms began to sweat, my muscles tightened, and the butterflies in my stomach flew. Anxiety had kicked in, and the voices inside my head told me that I wasn't good enough. The odd thing was that I often played in jazz combos with different musicians.

In fact, I'd been playing professionally in the U.S. Navy Band while freelancing with several bands around San Diego. So, this wasn't new for me. But for some reason, I doubted my abilities and talked myself out of playing that night. Instead, I decided to merely stay and listen to the band. After all, they were good, and I didn't want my night out to be for nothing. So, I took a seat in the corner to keep a low profile.

The band finished up their first set and went on break. I must've been giving off some kind of musician vibe from my secluded spot in the corner because the bass player (let's call him Billy) walked up to me and asked if I played. Caught off guard, I told him in a weak voice that I played bass. Damn it! My plan to lay low was not going well. Billy told me he'd ask his piano player (let's call him Lester) if I could sit in. As Billy walked away, I could feel my panic rising.

Billy returned a few minutes later with Lester, a talented pianist in his 70s with a permanent forehead crease. Needless to say, Lester took one look at me—the nervous wreck in the corner—and told Billy he wasn't down for a jam session with me. Aside from thinking his response was kind of rude, I was actually a bit relieved. This was my way out of having to play. But Billy wasn't ready to let it go. He insisted and, somehow, convinced Lester to give me a chance.

As I nervously took the stage and picked up the upright bass, I had a moment of clarity. I figured that all I needed to do was pick a song I was comfortable playing. I turned to Lester and said, "Hey, let's play *Stella by Starlight*," a standard jazz tune I knew from memory. Clearly annoyed, he grumpily informed me that they'd already played it. He then called a different tune that I didn't know at all. My anxiety went into overdrive as I fumbled through the music book to find the chart. Seconds later, Lester counted off the tune, and off we went.

By the time we reached the second chorus, disaster had struck. I got lost. Suddenly, jazz became foreign to me. I couldn't even figure out where we were in the music. I tensed up even more and simply started playing random notes. But there was no hiding. Lester eventually yelled out, "I need a real bass player." Then, Billy came on stage mid-song and took the bass from me. Humiliated in front of everyone, I fled the stage and made my way outside.

After that night, my self-confidence eventually became so shaken that I stepped away from music altogether. In fact, I stopped playing for eight years. Looking back, I can hardly believe I walked away for so long from something that I love so much.

But that's what fear can do to you. It can make you give up on your dreams, your passions, and your talents. That's why I wanted to write this book: to help musicians like you learn from my experiences in music and to give you the tools to be the performer you want to be.

I share this story as an example of how we can sabotage our own self-confidence. While that certainly wasn't my first (or last) time bombing a performance, it was certainly my most humiliating. Over the years, I played that night over and over again in my mind asking, "What could have gone differently?"

I eventually realized that *I* could have been different. I could've been more assertive with Billy and told him I wasn't going to play with anyone who didn't want to play with me. Or, I could've had the courage to tell Lester I'd only play tunes I know. But I didn't. Instead, I allowed others to control my performance. Avoiding that pitfall is a major lesson you'll learn from this book.

The other component that can sabotage us is our inner critic—that voice inside our head that creates self-doubt and anxiety. It's often a mask for our deepest fears, telling us we're not talented enough, smart enough, or pretty enough. Our inner critic is a mental block that, if left unmanaged, can destroy the self-confidence of even the most seasoned players.

Despite having played professionally for years, my inner critic flooded me that night in Los Angeles with reminders of all my past failures and mistakes. And, if that wasn't bad enough, the mental block spread throughout my whole body, causing my heart to race, my stomach to spasm, and my hands to shake and sweat.

And after it was all over, that night became one more failure for my inner critic to throw at me in future performances. That is, until I learned how to silence my inner critic, another tool you'll gain from this book.

I've played professionally for over 12 years with various pop and jazz bands from the West coast to the East coast. And no matter where I go, the number one issue I see among musicians is their struggle to quiet their inner critic. They're constantly beating themselves up, and that negative self-talk leads to performance anxiety and poor self-confidence. If you fall into this category, you aren't alone. Many musicians are right there with you.

After a long hiatus, I'm back into performing music. I learned how to turn my anxiety into excitement. I now look forward to playing and connecting with other musicians and audiences. I especially love getting called to play gigs with musicians I've never met before. Part of the adventure of being a musician isn't knowing what's going to happen but staying confident that it's going to work out. If you can learn to manage your anxiety and control your inner-critic, you'll gain the most from these new experiences, new music, and new musicians—all factors that lead to bigger and better playing opportunities.

Tune Up

Think about your inner voice. Is your inner critic holding you back from achieving your dreams in life or being the type of musician you would like to be? How can you quiet that voice and practice positive self-talk? What methods do you use to manage your anxiety as a musician?

CHAPTER 1

BORN WITH CONFIDENCE

We were all born with confidence. When we came out of the womb, we innately knew how to get what we wanted, before we could even speak. All we had to do was cry, and our parents would give us what we wanted. As babies, we did what we wanted until our parents told us to stop. We'd put objects in our mouths with no concern. We ran around naked with no shame. We flung ourselves across the monkey bars with no fear of falling.

Now, think back to when you first encountered a musical instrument. For most of us, we were kids at the time. And whatever instrument it was, I bet you weren't self-conscious about playing it. When you slammed the piano keys, you didn't know what the notes were. When you banged on the drums, you had no concept of time. When you blew the horn, you didn't know what an embrasure was. You simply played.

When I first picked up the bass guitar as a kid, I taught myself how to play Ben E. King's song *Stand by Me* by ear. But I played all the notes on one string because I didn't understand how to use the other strings, or what they were there for if one string could do the trick. And quite frankly, I didn't care if I was doing it right or not. I knew I was cool and could master this whole bass thing.

I bet you didn't have inhibitions as a child either. You were simply excited to be making music. And as far as you were concerned, you were a rock star in the making. Having this kind of confidence would have been great as you got older. But that's not what happened, is it?

Instead, most of you were enrolled in music lessons and were taught the "rules" (music theory). The rules confined you into parameters, forcing you to learn the "correct" way to play and proper technique. *Tune your instrument. Sit up straight. Slow down. Read the notes. Play your scales.*

Then, you enrolled in band class, and suddenly it wasn't all about you anymore. You had to restrain yourself and learn new rules to blend in with the other musicians. *Stop rushing. Play softer. Look at the conductor. Stop tapping your feet.*

As you continued on your journey of music, you may have hit other roadblocks that messed with your confidence. Trust me, I've hit them all. So, what really has the power to shake us? For most musicians, it's the rules, the environment, the dream suckers, and the awareness.

Rules

Learning and applying the rules (music theory) does, in fact, help us become better players. They are what keep everyone on the same sheet of music. Like language, you need to learn theory so that you can communicate with other musicians and have them understand you. And I'm telling you, you gain much more musical mileage having theory under your belt over musicians who don't.

A background in theory can also expose you to an infinite amount of possibilities and directions music can go, making you more adaptable to different musical situations. Let's take scales, for example. I've heard many non-theory and beginning musicians say the don't understand why they to .

learn scales.

But here's the big secret. Almost all music, including pop songs you hear on the radio, classical music, and jazz, are mostly based on some variation of scales. There are many ascending and descending uses of scales and arpeggios, even in the most complex songs. Now, I say almost all music because there are genres of music that hardly follow any rules (think the young kid banging on the drums), but, for the sake of time, we'll focus on the more "mainstream" genres in this book.

Proper technique can help prevent you from picking up bad habits that inevitability get in the way of progress. For example, if a horn player doesn't practice breathing properly, he or she may produce a shallow sound. Not learning proper technique can lead to a slew of bodily injuries that can affect your longevity of playing.

Now on to the downside of the rules. While learning theory can lead to liberation and self-discovery, it can also negatively affect your self-confidence. Music theory has so many nuances, that it can easily stress us out trying to figure out how and when to apply the rules. For example, classical players are focused on playing every note, articulation, and dynamic right while correctly interpreting the composer's work. Jazz players are focused on chord structures, improvising, and expanding their solo vocabulary. If the music doesn't come out the way we intended, our inner critic kicks in, and we become self-conscious.

Plus, once you've learned a new rule, it can take a while to apply it in a performance setting and make it sound natural. But it's human nature for us to want immediate results, and learning proper theory takes time. Many people can't handle the slow pace, and many of them give up playing music. It's important to understand and learn theory, without letting it drain you of all the reasons you started to play in the first place.

Environment

I was so excited the day I showed up to my duty station at Navy Band San Diego in July of 1996. I'd just graduated from the Naval School of Music in Little Creek, Virginia. My professional career was finally getting started. I was assigned to play in the Navy Band's Top 40 Band, the Jazz Band, and the Salsa Band. The bands consisted of the same exact musicians; they'd simply switch up the music for a given occasion. I thought it was cool that my job was to play different styles of music, and I was right where I wanted to be. Life couldn't get any better.

The commanding officer, who was the boss for the entire command, was filling in on bass guitar until I came aboard. When I arrived, he granted me a one-week free pass of not having to play. During that time, I followed the band around on their gigs and watched them play. Right off the bat, I was very intimidated. The band members were very experienced, most with over 10 years of professional playing under their belt. Some went on to play with famous musicians like Celia Cruz, Maynard Ferguson, and Tower of Power.

As for me, my professional career was only beginning. My lack of experience was evident during rehearsals and gigs. I was so worried about making mistakes that my anxiety made me mess up constantly. My bandmates were understandably frustrated and impatient with me. I'm sure most of them would have liked nothing more than for me to quit, give up on my dream, and never touch the bass again. I was clearly out of my element. I sucked, and I felt stupid and unsupported.

All of my time off was spent practicing to try to keep up with the other musicians. I began hating going to work every day, and my stomach would be in knots. But there was nowhere for me to go. I was under contract to play bass for Navy Band San Diego.

After a few months of this misery, the commanding officer decided to re-audition me due to all the complaints from my fellow bandmates. Talk about a tough environment— my own band didn't want to play with me! If I didn't pass, I'd be transferred out of the Navy Band and assigned to a non-musical job.

We played a few standard jazz tunes, and I actually played well. In the end, my commanding officer scratched his head and said, "You play fine. I don't get it." I didn't either! Looking back, I realize there were a couple of explanations for why I was not nervous that day. First, I practiced all the time, so I was naturally getting better. Second, I was playing with new band members during the re-audition, so none of that prior judgment was hanging over my head.

The re-audition was a great wakeup call for me. Even though being in the band was miserable at times, playing with more advanced musicians made me want to be better. The only thing left for me to do was to actually get better, and that I did.

Not long after my audition, a guitar player who was putting together a side band wanted me to play bass. I think he also realized how hard I was working and saw promise in me. I agreed to join because I knew that the more I played, the better I would get.

The band mostly consisted of local non-Navy musicians, and something remarkable happened when we started rehearsing. No one was on my case for messing up. In fact, no one was paying attention to me at all. The musicians were too worried about their own playing to notice my small, occasional mistakes. I felt so relieved, and music became fun to play again.

This was a turning point for me. I started playing more confidently with the Navy musicians and made vast improvements. Word of me spread in town, and I was hired by other bands.

Your external environment plays a big role in fueling, or fighting, your anxieties. Do what you need to in order to tune out the "noise" of the world and create a daily environment that inspires and nurtures your creativity. But sometimes, your environment is simply out of your control. You may be stuck in an unsupportive environment that stresses you out and amps up your anxieties. That's when it's really important to take notice and move toward positive change.

Dream Suckers

Our relationships with people are powerful influencers when it comes to shaping our feelings about ourselves. We allow the perception of those closest to us to affect our feelings and decisions. We seek their validation and worry over what they think of us. The problem with this is that they knowingly, or unknowingly, may try to talk us out of our dreams. If you know that people are blatantly trying to sabotage your forward-moving efforts, avoid them at all costs. Be careful about who you let in your circle and surround yourself with a positive environment of supportive friends and peers.

And if you do find yourself in the company of discouraging people, use it to fuel your motivation. Just like my first experience in the Navy Band, the very people who are (not so subtly) wishing you would give up on your dream may one day be asking you to play alongside them. Throughout your life, you'll encounter "dream suckers." Don't let them drag down your confidence. Instead, use it as a challenge to prove them wrong.

It's a little trickier dealing with people who unknowingly bring you down. These people actually care about you but may not realize the negative effect they're having on you. Due to their own insecurities or worries, they may feel threatened when they see you moving forward. They may come up with all kinds of "warnings" about why you shouldn't chase your dreams (it's too risky, you'll lose money, etc.).

But more often than not, these people are still struggling with their own fears. Do your best to recognize this and know that it's not about you. It doesn't mean you should ignore all of their advice, especially if they have good experience. Simply be mindful of the effect these people have on you. Keep looking for the areas in which you can continue to grow and chase your dreams—no matter what anyone else says.

Awareness

When I ask musicians where poor confidence stems from, the first thing they say is a lack of practice. While this may sound obvious, I'm amazed by the number of musicians who still show up to rehearsals and gigs unprepared. Many of these musicians eventually become flustered when they realize they can't make the cut. Some are lazy, and others simply don't know how to practice or work on their weak spots. (Chapters 6 and 7 will provide a method to help you properly prepare for rehearsals and performances.) Having an awareness of your destructive habits, such as a lack of preparation, can help you fight against them.

We can also be unaware of our own self-confidence problem. Our inner critic is so ingrained in us that many people are often unaware that they're putting up barriers or talking themselves out of great opportunities. If music teachers discount their own strengths, they inevitably pass that bad habit on to their students. Self-confidence isn't necessarily tied to a lack of ability. You can do all the practicing in the world and still have your confidence knocked down by the unrealistic bar of excellence that you set for yourself. We want the music to sound perfect every time, but that's not how life works. Humans inevitably make mistakes; it's how we learn. If you aren't making mistakes sometimes, you aren't challenging yourself. Growing is about taking risks, but you need to have the confidence to do it.

Unfortunately, there isn't much material that addresses musicians' inner critic and how to quiet it. We need to reprogram our brains to undo this negative habit. But to effectively do this, we need to look at the underlying problem—fear.

Tune Up

- Are rules, your environment, dream suckers, or your lack of awareness causing you the most harm right now? If so, how can you create a healthier balance in those areas?
- What unrealistic expectations might you be putting yourself under? What unrealistic expectations might others be putting on you?

CHAPTER 2

THE ROOT CAUSE

We need to rebuild self-confidence. But before we can do that, we have to discover the root cause of our fears. Fear is an emotion we feel when there's a perceived danger, because one of our basic needs as humans is to feel safe. We feel the need to protect our vulnerabilities so that they aren't exposed.

I was once hired to play a jazz gig by a very talented saxophonist whom I had played with before. The cats he played with were advanced, had graduate music performance degrees, and had full-time musical careers. I was an intermediate-level player, playing music on the side of my non-musical day job. This was a great way for me to step it up. Plus, my hope was to meet more people who would thrust me into other musicians' networks so that I could get hired for more gigs.

Right off the bat, I was out of my comfort zone. The sax player requested to play *Giant Steps* by John Coltrane. I gulped. If you aren't familiar with this song, it's arguably one of the hardest jazz standards to play. It's almost as if all the rules and theory you ever learned about jazz are thrown out the window, leaving you clueless about how to improvise over this tune. That's why most beginner and intermediate jazz musicians, including myself, shy away from playing it. But, I was determined to face my fear and "prove" myself, so I sucked it up and got ready to play.

Before counting off the tune, the sax player decided to start with a solo, and then, have the band come in later. Off he went, while I was busy thinking about how I'd have no clue when to jump in. And that's exactly what happened when the sax player cued us in.

To make matters worse, the band was playing at lightning speed, way faster than I could handle. I was sweating bullets. It was, officially, a train wreck, and I caused it. Finally, the tune ended, mainly because the song had come so far off the tracks that we couldn't recover. I was relieved but embarrassed.

Trying to salvage my pride, I decided to call a common song—*Yardbird Suite* by Charlie Parker. I was surprised when the ultra-experienced sax player told me he didn't know it. When he said that, a part of me thought, "Ha! You don't know everything either." But then, I quickly realized that he didn't have to know everything, and neither did I.

When he called *Giant Steps*, I should have said I didn't know it. Those simple words could have averted disaster. But my ego got in the way. I was too worried about being seen as not good enough when, in reality, the sax player hired me because he liked the way I played. But because I chose to mask my fear with ego, it cost me. I never got called back.

That experience helped me see how my ego and fears hold me back. Now, I'm always working to keep them in check. I don't have to make it about me. I'm there to contribute to the group, foster an environment of creativity, and have fun. I try to approach every musical project with that in mind. I don't have to be the star. I'm merely working on the formula to produce good music and leave my ego at the door. I've found that this starts by understanding your fear.

Fear is a tricky emotion. There are many types of fears, and they can mask themselves in many ways, usually without us even realizing it. Here are some common fears associated with music—and life in general.

Fear of Failure

Failure is probably the biggest fear among musicians. If you've ever experienced a big "failure," it's easy to get disillusioned and think it's the end of the world. It's what keeps people in their comfort zones and prevents them from wanting to try again. Some people refrain from experimenting and only engage in efforts that guarantee a "successful" outcome. These people may think perfectionism is a necessary element for mastery, but it isn't. If you chase perfection, you'll only end up chasing something that doesn't exist.

Take it from me; failure in itself isn't necessarily a bad thing. It's the fear of failure that trips us up. Failure is inevitable, so we should accept it. Taking chances, making mistakes, and applying lessons learned is the most effective way we grow and build confidence. You certainly need to still put your best effort into practicing and being prepared in order to take the fear out of failure. That way, when you make a mistake, you can feel good knowing that you've still done your best.

Fear of Rejection

One of our basic needs as humans is to feel that we belong. When we belong, we feel as if we matter and are contributing to something purposeful. However, people are always judging, which makes us constantly worry that we aren't good enough. We don't want to have our shortcomings exposed. So, we seek others' acknowledgment, approval, and acceptance. We strive to live up to their expectations so that they won't reject us.

One way we avoid rejection is by getting people to lower their expectation of us so that we don't have to reach higher. I knew a guy who had been playing professionally for three years. But when he got in front of the audience, he'd tell them he was a beginner player—to lower their expectations and then blow them away when the "beginner" turned out to be an experienced player.

If you're guilty of this, or other manipulations to make yourself belong, you may have a fear of rejection that you need to address. You'll waste a lot of energy worrying over what others may or may not be thinking about you. Who cares? Take that energy and focus on doing what you love. If they like it, that's great. If they don't, then move on. You're not for everyone, and everyone isn't for you.

Fear of Humiliation

Humiliation is an extremely powerful fear. We have a basic need for others to see us as significant, and being humiliated takes that significance away. Humiliation shows up in all kinds of ways. It's a feeling of shame and a personal violation of our boundaries. Some intensely painful humiliating experiences can lead to stage fright, which can be a debilitating fear. In fact, there are many famous people who have been performing for a long time and still suffer from stage fright. (Barbara Streisand, Chaka Khan, Carly Simon, and Rod Stewart are among notable the names we could list.)

When we're humiliated, our "fight or flight" instinct kicks in. We immediately want to escape the embarrassing situation. The shame may be so intense that avoidance is the only solution we can think of in the moment. But the fear doesn't go away. Eventually, it backs us into a corner where we feel as if we can't do anything without being humiliated. This means you are less likely to take chances, try new experiences, or take on challenging opportunities.

Like rejection, humiliation is a fear that's rooted in other people. We only feel humiliation or shame as a result of how we think others perceive us. Once we start to move past caring about that perception, we can let go of humiliation, and embrace ourselves more fully.

Fear of the Unknown

Fear of the unknown is nerve-racking for musicians because it puts us out of our comfort zone. After leaving the military, I was forced to make it on my own, without the comfort of a steady military check. As soon as I found my own place, the fear of the unknown started to creep in. I wasn't sure how I was going to cover the rent and other bills. I didn't know if I could make it as a full-time musician and was worried that I would have to move back in with my parents if I failed. So, I got to work. I had many side jobs at the time, from being an extra in movies to a courier for the entertainment business to selling knives—anything I could do to support myself. While I had several unknowns, going through that experience thickened my skin and made me self-reliant in a totally new way.

In a performance setting, musicians who fear the unknown probably aren't comfortable playing improvisation. They don't want to deviate from the music because they might make a mistake. However, success is never guaranteed, and the unknowns will always leave us with a sense of not being in control. Even little unknowns, such as worrying about finding a new venue or a parking spot close to the entrance so that we can unload our equipment, can throw us off.

The problem with eliminating all of the unknowns is that it would rob you of the experience, and the excitement, of the journey. You don't get the experience of the hustle. Or the determination, passion, and tireless efforts to get your music to the masses. You miss the thick skin you develop when you keep trying, after many rejections, until you reach your goal. And you can't help guide other musicians through the process because you lack the experience yourself. The "unknown" is a part of life's journey. It may not be what you expect, but the beauty is learning and experiencing the success and failures along the way. Most importantly, you build self-confidence, gain wisdom, and learn a lot about yourself.

Tune Up

- Think about a musical opportunity you could have taken advantage of but chose to pass up. It could have been a jam session, an audition, or some other type of musical project. Why did you pass on it? Try going deeper than the excuses you gave other people for not participating. What was the fear that held you back?

CHAPTER 3

OVERCOMING BAD HABITS

As musicians, we have a lot going on in our heads when it comes to performing. The fear of failure, rejection, humiliation, and the unknown can lead to bad habits that keep us in a cycle of fear. Our fear behaviors become automatic, plaguing our ability to improve our self-confidence. Chronic bad habits can take on many different forms, making it more challenging for us to undo them and progress in our music goals.

Once you begin to diagnose your fears, you'll also start to become more aware of the bad habits that surround those fears. As we react to fear, we fall into patterns of behavior that can really hurt who we are as musicians and as people. Here are some of the most common habits fear can make us turn to, and how you can start to break out of them.

Excuses

We've all been there—giving some excuse about why we simply *can't* practice. Even worse, we've probably all been on the receiving end of a lame excuse from a friend or bandmate.

Lame excuses are easy to detect because there are obvious solutions to them. For example, "I was so busy this week that I didn't have time to practice." In reality, a person always finds time for what really matters. Practicing simply may not be on the top of the list.

I used to be in a band in which the singer would come up with all kinds of excuses as to why he couldn't practice the songs. So, he showed up to rehearsals not knowing the tunes. He was forever forgetting the words during the gig. We'd spend several hours in rehearsal not progressing because we were repeating songs over and over again until he memorized them. The band finally came to a consensus to have him replaced.

We need to be mindful that we aren't avoiding our fears by making excuses. They're merely our habit of letting life get in the way. We subconsciously put reasons that are valid in front of what we are trying to do. Suddenly, trying to achieve that goal has become complicated—so complicated that it gives a reason not to do it. This is letting life get in the way. This is a huge and important habit to notice because it is tricky when dealing with it in yourself and from others. The most common music-related excuses tend to fall into a few major categories:

I'm too busy.

Saying you don't have enough time makes another subtle but severe impact on moving you forward. It's a common, roll-off-the-tongue thing to say when we don't want to meet deadlines. It's automatic and habitual. But you can always make time for what really matters to you. You need to figure out what is most important and to prioritize them. Maybe you go to bed 10 minutes later and wake up 10 minutes earlier. Boom! You now have 20 minutes you can dedicate to moving yourself toward your goal.

I'm not good enough.

This is a common excuse to keep you in your comfort zone. But to grow, we have to go outside of our comfort zone. You don't have to take a big leap. You can take baby steps like I did by finding one or two people who will practice with you. Try out new music that pushes the envelope for you. I'm definitely a stronger and less fearful player as a result of embracing risk. And remember, don't chase perfection! It doesn't exist.

It's too difficult.

I'm not saying being a musician is easy. It's actually not about whether it's hard or easy. It's all about having the patience to work on the craft and stick around for the results. The results aren't always immediate, which is why many people get impatient and quit. They don't realize that improving on any instrument is all about repetition. That's it! That's the big secret to learning to play an instrument—starting slow and then, gradually getting faster and more proficient until, eventually, what you're playing comes naturally. It's about persistence and the willingness to keep trying when you have setbacks.

I'm too old to learn.

Any mentally competent person with working limbs who can position themselves on the instrument can learn to play. While some people learn faster than others and some have an affinity to it at a young age, much of it comes down to muscle memory. So, if you want to learn, now is the perfect time. Get yourself some instructional books, videos, or a teacher, and get to work.

If you realize that you aren't where you want to be in your musical career, take a look at your excuses. I have to do this all the time when I feel that I'm not moving forward. I have to really make sure I'm being honest with myself and not putting other things before my main priorities either consciously or unconsciously.

Even as I write this book, I always have to revisit why I keep falling behind schedule for getting it done. Bottom line: if something is important to you, whether it's music or writing a book or spending more time with people you love, stop making excuses and start taking small actions every day to further your priorities.

Masking

We don't like to be told we're wrong, and we'll blame everyone and everything but ourselves to avoid it. I once played in a band in which I was one of the more inexperienced players. At one point, the singer stopped the song because of a train wreck of a mistake one of us had made. I heard it, too, but flat out denied that it was me. I rejected the notion that I could've made the mistake. But, through fault isolation, everyone figured out that I was, indeed, at fault. I wasn't paying enough attention and ended up in a different spot in the music. My ego was bruised—both for having made the mistake and for my inability to take constructive criticism.

Our egos determine how and when to mask our fears. Whether consciously or unconsciously, this happens a lot. The problem is that the mask can distort our perceptions. Ego puts up blinders, keeping us self-absorbed and unable to empathize with others and see different viewpoints. So, we rationalize illogical decisions at the expense of others. Sometimes, we convince others to take our side to boost our own ego. These masks can destroy relationships, end careers, and wreak all kinds of havoc.

Over-Confidence

Over-confidence isn't self-confidence. It's a distorted view of ourselves that inhibits our ability to think clearly. This stems from not keeping our egos in check, which can lead to reckless behavior that eventually exposes your weakness.

Let's say, for example, that a band's piano player is unavailable for a gig next month. So, you get hired to fill in. You practice the music over and over again to get it down. You play well in band practice and at the gig. Fellow bandmates tell you what a great player you are and how well you performed. This gives you a big boost of confidence. So, you decide you don't need to practice the music for the next gig with them. You tell yourself you've got this. After all, you impressed everyone last time.

But this time, you don't perform so well because you've forgotten some of the hits and stops during the songs. Your secret is out. You didn't practice, and everyone knows it. Your over-confidence has sabotaged the gig. Not practicing was a missed opportunity for you to maintain and improve your skills and make the music sound even better this time around. Always remember that there are plenty of other players who are just as good as you, if not more so, and who can take your place. Confidence draws people to you. Arrogance pushes them away.

Tune Up

Think about a forward-moving situation you were in that you feared. What were the excuses you used to get you out of it? How has this held you back?

CHAPTER 4

REBUILDING CONFIDENCE

During the late 1990s, I began developing a problem that would take me out of commission from playing music for eight years. I got excited every time people called me for a gig. It meant other people thought I was worthy enough to play with, and I was happy to be making my living performing music.

But eventually, I found myself getting butterflies leading up to a gig. Over time, the butterflies became more intense. My stomach would cramp up and I would feel faint. I didn't understand what was going on. I was playing all the time and building nerves of steel. Yet I was experiencing these symptoms.

It was starting to become a real problem for me, so much so that as soon as I accepted a gig, I would come up with ways to get out of it. And the more advanced notice I received, the worse I'd stress and obsess over not wanting to play. But I still didn't know why. I kept trying to think about the kind of music I wanted to play that would give me joy, but everything was looking bleak.

Playing music had become a real drag. When I was on the gig, all I could think about was how much I wanted to be in the comfort of my own home. If I was performing in a place that had a TV, I'd watch it while I played to keep myself entertained and distracted from what I was feeling. I was completely disinterested in the music.

Then, I thought about the compensation. I'd ask myself how much money someone would have to offer for me to want to do a gig. At first, it was a thousand dollars. Then, the number grew and grew, all the way to a million. Eventually, it moved to zero. There was no amount of money that made playing music feel worth it. That's when I knew I had to walk away.

I let this go on for so long that I became bitter about the whole playing experience. I sold my basses and amplifiers and threw out the rest of my equipment and every music book I owned. I didn't want any of it in my presence. I couldn't even stand hearing songs on the radio that I used to play.

When I told people I was giving up music, they were shocked and thought it was coming out of nowhere. But no one was as shocked as I was to have gotten to this point. I never thought I'd stop playing music. My musician friends and I always had the attitude that it was us musicians against the world.

After I gave up music, I felt relieved. But soon, I noticed that my nervousness began occurring outside of the music world. I got nervous when friends wanted me to hang out. I'd always try to find excuses to get out of it. I'd do something like stage to have a friend call me and pretend his car was broken down and that he was stranded on the side of the road. I'd say, "Sorry, I need to go and help a friend in need." Ridiculous! But what I didn't realize at the time was that I had social phobia. Social phobia is a type of anxiety that involves a fear of being in social settings.

It would take three years after I quit music for me to figure that out. It would take me another five years of learning how to manage it before returning to music. I stopped enjoying playing music because it meant I had to be around people. I thought the problem had something to do with music, but when I got an office job, I noticed that it was pretty painful simply to say hello to people on my way to my desk in the morning. (I still get that feeling, but I've learned how to manage it.) That's when I finally began to realize my problems were bigger than music alone.

The road to rebuilding confidence won't be easy. It may cause you to realize that the true root of your fear isn't what you thought it was. It may have many twists and turns along the way. It may even take you eight years to do it. But I promise you, it's worth it. And you can start the journey today.

Building Self-Esteem

Fear is a natural instinct that everyone feels at some point. There are many types of fear with their own various dimensions and complexities. How much we let them get in the way of reaching our potential depends on our level of self-esteem. To have high self-esteem is to feel good about yourself and to know your worth.

Low self-esteem, on the other hand, may manifest itself in self-loathing and not feeling good enough, or having low expectations of life and yourself. It's judging ourselves by what others think and looking for them to give us self-esteem. Learning how to deal with your negative thoughts is an effective way of starting to boost your self-esteem.

High self-esteem is the foundation for self-confidence. Self-confidence is situational and fleeting, while self-esteem remains consistent through up and down times. Therefore, we want to work on improving our self-esteem to change the destructive behaviors that result from fear and low self-confidence. That's not to say that if you have high self-esteem, you won't feel fear. But improving our self-esteem can reduce our fears and provide us with self-confidence to be more effective in meeting our goals.

Turning Anxiety Around

Anxiety generally stems from fear. It can make us self-conscious in every move we make. Of course, we can't overcome every physical, mental, or emotional anxiety. But we certainly have a level of control we can tap into so that we can still move and groove with confidence. There are opportunities in every mishap no matter how small. It's up to us to find them and manage the rest. The worst thing you can do is succumb to hopelessness.

The first step to turning anxiety around is holding yourself accountable for any part of the situation you can control. If time is a challenge for you, take stock of what you're doing throughout the day. Have you prioritized your tasks? Do you have too much on your plate? Are you working through your tasks efficiently?

Try eliminating anything in your day that isn't moving you forward. Acknowledge and figure out ways to take advantage of opportunities. I've also discovered ways to help reduce stress when playing music. I've done quite a bit of self-work to get to this point, and you may need to also.

Fighting Depression

I fell into a deep episode of depression in the early days of trying to figure out my anxiety issue. It was a very dark time for me that seemed impossible to overcome. It consumed me to the point that I didn't have the capacity to hold a job. Even a simple walk to the mailbox became a huge task. It required me to do a lot of mental preparation. While I was awake, the pain was so deep that I spent most of my days crying. I hated going to sleep because I always had vivid dreams of abandonment and was left feeling terrible when I woke up. I turned to alcohol to numb the pain. Eventually, I sought help from a therapist. I think anyone who is battling with depression, anxiety, or another mental illness should do the same. You can't, and don't need to, fight this on your own.

I was desperate for immediate relief and didn't want to wait for a prescription to kick in. So, my therapist taught me a simple yet effective tool: count the number of steps it takes to walk to the mailbox and back. Staying focused on the counting kept me distracted enough from the pain to get the task done. Then, the light bulb went off.

I didn't have to be paralyzed. I could find ways to keep distracted and take my mind off the sadness while I was working on healing. I put my pride aside and told a friend who wanted nothing more than to help. He started including me in short trips to the grocery store and other errands. It doesn't sound like a big deal, but it gave me something to look forward to and got me out of the house. The distracting method worked for me most of the time. And when it didn't, I made sure to work my way up to tasks that felt too overwhelming. In the end, you're the only one who knows your capacity.

Knowing Your Capacity

My anxiety used to limit my social and professional life, and sometimes, it still does. However, through trial and error over time, I've learned to be more in tune with my stress levels and understand what I can and can't take on. We all have a capacity threshold. Knowing where that threshold lays will determine your ability to handle your career, and life, as a musician. Everything we take on, from big to the small, eats away at our capacity. The more maxed out your capacity is, the less you're able to take on more and succeed. If you're at max capacity, you should look at ways of freeing up some room to avoid becoming stressed out or having a nervous breakdown.

You also need to recognize that your capacity adjusts whenever your given situation changes, so it's constantly moving. For example, your boss may assign you a huge project and only give you two days to complete it. At work, you're stressing out. Then. on your way home from work, you listen to your favorite song on the radio. This helps relieve some of your stress in that moment. Whether you realize it or not, that small break has given you more capacity to deal with whatever additional stressors come at you. This is why it's so important to separate your work from your life and create daily habits that help you decompress.

To re-build confidence, we need to break old negative habits and develop new productive ones. All musicians, even the most advanced, need to do this continually in order to grow. So, we need something in place to continually build self-esteem and confidence. Through accountability, planning, practicing, challenging myself and my physiology, I've improved my playing confidence, my mental health, and my overall happiness.

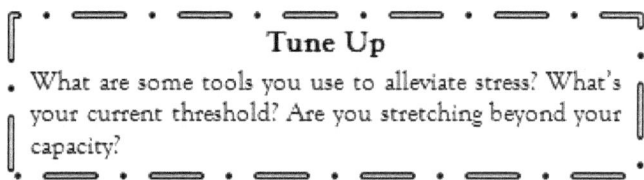

Tune Up

What are some tools you use to alleviate stress? What's your current threshold? Are you stretching beyond your capacity?

CHAPTER 5

OWNERSHIP AND ACCOUNTABILITY

Whether you realize it or not, fear doesn't happen without your consent. You can gain control and kick it in the ass. The first step is to hold yourself accountable and take ownership of everything holding you back. Ownership and accountability are about being brave and facing your fears to fix issues.

That also means having the courage to admit your role in a given situation, no matter how painful it may be. A key step to this is to stop blaming others and everything else for how you're feeling, and work toward acceptance. I look at ownership and accountability in three steps: accept yourself, accept others, and accept the situation.

Accept Yourself

Being accountable starts with accepting ourselves. This means accepting our capabilities and limitations with your current level as a musician. Of course, accepting our capabilities is easy—after all, highlighting our strengths makes us feel good. Accepting our limitations is tougher because we don't like to have our vulnerabilities exposed. This fear is so ingrained in us that our fear-induced behaviors are automatic in helping us to avoid exposure.

The first step in breaking this habit is to be aware that you're doing it. The second step, which is probably the hardest, is to admit you're covering up your fears and to accept you need to change. This requires being humble and accepting that you're not perfect. Then, you need to ask yourself what is it that you're afraid of and what is triggering your anxiety. Once you can identify the fears, you can find your anxiety triggers and arm yourself with information to pull yourself out of fear.

It took me a long time to figure out that I have a social phobia. I knew that I was avoiding performances and covering it up. I was actually pretty embarrassed to admit that I had limitations. My ego was telling me that I was too good of a player to have limitations. So, when I left music, I'd always tell myself and other people that I was simply burned out on music and needed a break.

Because I told myself this lie, I closed myself off from looking at what I really feared. It wasn't until I noticed that I was engaging in the same fear-based behavior (avoiding going to parties, the movies, work) regarding other social events that I realized that it wasn't about music at all.

When you get into the habit of accepting your limitations, the painful feeling begins to dissipate, and you no longer feel the need to cover them up. Accept your role in the process, and work on turning your limitation into a capability. Let's say your band stops a song during rehearsal because a mistake was made and you know you made it. Own up to it. Humans make mistakes, and people will respect you for taking ownership. Then, work out your part and make it better.

You may need to look at how prepared you are before rehearsal and spend more time rehearsing by yourself. I've certainly done this myself. (We'll walk through rehearsal prep in the next few chapters.) You need to accept and own your part so that you can do your best. It takes a lot of practice to establish this habit, and it's ongoing. But every time you do it, it eats away at your fear and strengthens your confidence.

Forgiveness is another important part of self-acceptance. Forgive yourself for your past mistakes and know that it's okay to continue to make them. The greatest musicians make them all the time. I love the song *More Love* by Victor Wooten, a modern-day bass pioneer. I recently watched an online video of him playing the song live but at a faster tempo than the version recorded on his album. During the song, he made an obvious mistake. He played a wrong note that was outside of the scale and not part of the melody. If that wasn't obvious enough, Victor let out a growl, which let everyone know that the note he played was unintended.

But the wrong note didn't end his career. Instead, he continues to excel and innovate what can be played on the bass. If musicians at the highest levels can make mistakes, then musicians at any other levels can too. I'd encourage you to watch your favorite musicians play live. They all make mistakes at some point or another. Sometimes, they're obvious; other times, you'll never know. Either way, making them is an effective way of learning. Identifying what went wrong, correcting it, and applying lessons learned can have you come out better than you have before. In addition to improved confidence, you gain valuable experience and wisdom. Don't hold the mistakes against yourself. Forgive, learn, and move on.

Accept Others

Accept other musicians as you'd accept yourself. Accept their abilities, limitations, and current skill level. Finding the good in your fellow musicians is always a positive choice. It means you've taken down your negative blinders and have a clearer view of who that person is and what they bring to the table. It really speaks to your character when you find something nice to say about someone. When you make people feel good, they want to hang around you.

I once was in a band that required a vocalist to sing in a soprano range. People, including myself, complained that she couldn't sing. But when I stepped back and listened, I realized she had a very pretty way of singing songs in the alto range. She was an alto singer, not a soprano. So, we leveraged her strength and stuck to playing songs that were in her range. And she did a beautiful job singing them.

Determine how you can grow with every musician. We should strive to open ourselves up to gain from other musicians. Part of accepting others is realizing that we all learn and process information differently—providing a wide array of perspectives. This is one of life's greatest beauties, because knowing those different perspectives helps us grow from each other even further.

Our role is to help our fellow musicians. We do this by encouraging and promoting trust so that they feel comfortable about their playing. Unless you're auditioning for a musical role, don't try to show them up. It's unnecessary and makes it obvious that you're insecure. Most of the time, people try to make a big deal about me being a female bassist in a male-dominated arena.

Usually, I get mistaken for being the vocalist, something I'm sure other female musicians deal with. You could say that it puts pressure on me and makes me feel as if I have to prove myself. But I don't feel the need to get wrapped up in the hype. I try to stick to playing with forward-moving musicians who maintain a good vibe. In those settings, I forget my gender because I'm not thinking about it. It's irrelevant. I accept other musicians regardless of gender identity, and I hope that they do the same for me.

That isn't to say that I never experience sexism, because I definitely do. I experience it in and out of the music world. I keep my distance from sexist musicians and sexist audience members. Still, I accept that they have some insecurity about themselves. They never get me down, and I'm able to remain positive. Instead of plotting to get revenge, I'm plotting to get to my best musical self and help others do the same.

Accept the Situation

You can't control the cards you're dealt. But you can control your reaction toward situations. The first step in dealing with unpleasant situations is accepting that things often happen that are beyond your control. It's impossible to plan for everything that you will come across. Situations don't always turn out the way we expect them to. Sometimes, we are met with great opportunities we didn't expect, such as coming into money, meeting someone famous, or getting a record deal.

Then, there are situations where the benefits aren't as apparent. But know that they're there and that we have to look for them. To find them, we first must ensure our negative blinders are down. Let's say a professional player is asked to play with an elementary school band for charity. One of the student's parents sitting in the audience just happens to be a successful talent scout looking for musicians to play on the next Janet Jackson album. Talk about unexpected benefits! Or maybe a musician you played with a year earlier calls on you for a good-paying, steady gig. You never know where a situation will lead, so acceptance is your best option.

This isn't to say that you should say yes to every situation. I recently turned down an opportunity from a fellow bass player to replace him in an original pop band. As much as I liked the opportunity, my capacity for taking on musical projects was maxed. And at the end of the day, the benefit wasn't enough to take me away from my main priorities—including finishing this book!

The more you take ownership and hold yourself accountable, the more you start focusing on what you can control and less on how other people and situations are controlling you. I hold myself accountable for whatever I'm feeling before, during, and after a performance. I apply this to all facets of my life in taking control of my reaction and letting go what I can't change. You really need to limit how much others are to blame. We may be able to influence others, but we can't control them. So, why waste your energy?

When you start holding yourself accountable, you become more empowered because you give yourself the power to turn things around. Get in the driver's seat. Don't be a passenger in your own life.

Tune Up

What's the hardest thing for you to accept—yourself, others, or your situation? What are you doing to move toward acceptance? How do you hold yourself accountable for your playing?

CHAPTER 6

PLAN

When I conducted research on how musicians plan for gigs, almost all of the results I found were no more than guides on booking a gig or organizing events. I could barely find any information on how to plan for a performance from the perspective of each individual musician. After all, the onus is on each of us to do our part individually. Maybe this trait is thought of as inherent, because the goal of being prepared and having a successful show is so obvious.

Obvious or not, the planning phase gives you the chance to get in front of fears associated with performing. It also motivates you to stay on top of practicing and the logistics associated with the gig. You are essentially managing fear, and it is not managing you. If you want a successful outcome, look at the bigger picture. That starts with being aware of how much prep work is needed and the amount of time you need to get it done. This planning phase is a very necessary step before we start practicing. Yet, so many people neglect it.

Some may think it isn't necessary, silly, or have simply never thought of it.

Whatever the case may be, those who don't plan will likely procrastinate. Procrastination puts you into crisis mode, leaving you trying to learn tunes at the last minute. Another common mistake musicians make is focusing too much on one area and not enough on others. They practice what they already know and don't pay enough attention to the stuff that needs focused work. This leads to plateauing, because they're not progressing their weaker skills. You're only as strong as your weakest spot. So, it's important to give those areas more of your attention.

Planning is vital because there is so much to learn in music, and it can easily leave you feeling very overwhelmed and flustered. In order to have a successful outcome, visualize the bigger picture, your end goal, and develop a game plan for how you're going to get there. Planning is doing all the prep work needed to execute the performance as smoothly as possible.

While the key to getting in front of your fears is to take action upfront and early, you still need to start by knowing what effective action to take. To prepare is to organize, set goals, set timelines, and establish an execution plan. Creating a plan allow you to identify potential issues and risks so that they don't' become problems and crises, leaving you to fly by the seat of your pants. Planning can be as long or as short as you need it to be. The important thing is to do it because it will make your practice sessions more productive in getting you prepared for the performance. These steps are all part of gaining confidence. Here are some tools to help you plan for successful outcomes in music. These tools can also be applied to other areas in life.

Step 1 - Organize
If you're performing all the time, you know how important it is to stay organized. You need to keep your dates straight so that you don't double book yourself and so that

you know when to show up. You also need to keep the music organized and have the time to prepare for each performance. As soon as you know about the event, immediately put the date on your calendar. Even if a potential gig arises, put in on the calendar as tentative. Gather all the information needed and write it down! Keep it in one spot, in an organized way.

Staying organized prevents information that you might not remember from falling through the cracks. Don't waste people's time by asking repeat questions they've already answered. Even if it's a gig in which you only have to play one song, learning that one tune isn't the only thing you have going on in your daily schedule. You still need to fit this around your other life tasks. So, always write everything down and take the time to prepare—even for a "simple" show.

If you're the one booking the gig, communicate with all parties involved proactively about what's going to happen. The pertinent information is the pay, date, time, location, and list of songs. Even if you don't have all the details yet, giving them a heads up goes a long way. You can follow up with them later with the finer details.

I get called for some gigs that pretty much only ask me to show up without much information, not even a list of the songs sometimes. The musicians are stuck finding their way around by trial and error. This drives many people crazy. Adding this stress on top of the existing stress of performance is nerve-wracking. If you are the one booking a gig, don't do this to your fellow musicians. Be thorough, do your homework, and let everyone involved know the important information, including where to park and unload your equipment, points of contact, and the song list in advance.

Step 2 – Set Goals

Now that you have the pertinent information you need, the next step is to set your goals. An obvious goal is for you to know your part and execute a successful performance. Obvious or not, setting goals isn't enough. You have to write them down. WRITE THEM DOWN. This is the most common step that people blow off. The fact is you're likely to accomplish goals if they're written down. It's a simple trick to keep you focused on your priorities.

Merely keeping goals in your head leaves you vulnerable to getting sidetracked when other things are thrown at you. You begin to reprioritize, putting other things first. This leads to procrastination, last minute cramming, wasted time, and showing up unprepared. Your goals are also easier to move and edit in your head, letting yourself off the hook for not reaching them. Written goals don't move unless you physically change them. Your goals can be focused on specific gigs or on your career at large. They should be things that you're passionate about and excited to achieve.

Step 3 - Draw a Roadmap

It's not enough to merely set goals. A critical step to achieving any goal is a roadmap to get you there. I hear people say all the time, "I want (fill in the blank)." But I hardly ever hear them finish that statement with, "and here's how I'm going to get there." They don't have a plan. You can't hit a target you can't see. And, your chances to hit that target are only as good as your aim, or plan.

I learned the art of prioritization via my current day job. It's a fast-paced environment in which I manage various projects at once. Each project consists of many tasks with each having their own deadlines. In order to meet these deadlines, I have to ensure that each task is progressing. To do this, I set milestones and write the due dates next to each task. I then prioritize my list based on the due date and put more focus on the top critical task.

When you have your goals and plan written down, you can also communicate better with others. If you're leading a band and setting the tunes and rehearsals, it keeps everyone on the same page. Lead musicians who don't do this will usually send you a list of 100 songs when you only need to know 30 for the show. This wastes rehearsal time and makes it nearly impossible for you to draw your roadmap to success.

Unfortunately, this is the reality with many leaders. So, you will need to take ownership. If you need clarity, ask for it. Do whatever you need to in order to have the tools to draw your roadmap to success.

Step 4 - Create a Timeline

The next step is to set a timeline for your roadmap. There is no one-size-fits-all timeline because it depends on how much advance notice you have and the priorities of other areas in your life. But the closer you are to the rehearsal and gig, the more your timeline should move toward the top of your priority list. As I'm writing this chapter, I have several upcoming gigs for which I have to learn music. I prioritize which ones I need to learn first while allotting enough time for the more complex tunes that take longer to learn.

Even as you're prioritizing the list, you're also prioritizing everything else you have going on with your life. So, your timeline should be realistic. Don't take on more than you can handle. It's not enough to simply write it down. Sticking to the timeline is the hardest part. It's easy to let life get in the way. Suddenly, you can find yourself off track and missing deadlines because you let yourself become consumed with other tasks.

I've seen people set timelines, but then, they are too stubborn to not deal with tasks that get thrown their way. They can't say no and usually end up getting off track with the original priority. This is a bad habit to get into because it will show up every time, and you will chronically miss deadlines.

I've seen people show up to rehearsals, and even gigs, unprepared countless times. The lack of practice is most likely due to the lack of proper planning. I certainly have been guilty of not managing my life's tasks properly and have found myself winging it. I've shown up to rehearsals flustered, unprepared, and making fundamental mistakes. It always leaves me embarrassed for not having my stuff together. I waste people's time because we have to keep stopping and playing it again until I nail it. That is, if I'm lucky enough to get a rehearsal in. Otherwise, I'm just making mistakes during the gig.

Don't be that person. It's a selfish way to carry on because it wastes other members' time as well as the audience if you put on a lackluster performance. It also sends the message that you don't care enough about the music quality to have your part down. If you've ever been guilty of this, you should trace your steps backward to see what led up to that point of unpreparedness. By not doing the investigative work to get to the root cause, you become comfortable with the path of least resistance, and it becomes a habit. Most people are prone to choosing the path of least resistance. They want the success without the pain of working for it. So, they will do the least amount of work to get there. Always put in the work. You will never regret it.

Step 5 - Get to Know Your Music

I recommend memorizing tunes as much as possible versus solely rely on reading charts. Doing so gets you more intimate with the music and frees you up to listen more closely to the other musicians, connecting with them and the audience. You can be flexible and more adaptable to on-the-spot changes. The more you know, the more flexible you are to adapt to any given situation. To accelerate your growth in flexibility, you have to challenge yourself constantly so that you can expand your capabilities. So, don't let any musical situation pass you by without grabbing some kind of opportunity that helps you grow.

For example, before every gig, I always identify something I will do differently or incorporate something I can do to challenge myself. This also keeps the playing experience exciting for me because I never played it like I did on previous performances. In some bands, when the leader isn't present, or there is no clear leadership, I step up and fulfill the role. It isn't always stated. But typically, the leadership role will gravitate toward the person that knows the material and speaks up to help move the band forward.

Sometimes, I see musicians who are buried in their music stand and never look up. It could be because they are sight-reading or worried about messing up. The audience and your fellow bandmates are less likely to connect with you, and you may have a tougher time getting your part to sync and blend with the other musicians. The music suffers because it can't breathe and doesn't groove. This is why it's even more important to address your nervousness.

Why would anyone want to listen to someone who is self-absorbed? Ask yourself that when the audience doesn't clap, smile, bob their heads, or respond to what you're playing. If you're performing, you should make it about your audience just as much as you make it about yourself. With bandmates, that's part of being in a band. It's a team effort, even if you're a solo act performing for people. It's a team effort in that there is an exchange of energy between you and the audience.

I understand there are exceptions to this. Examples would be jazz, big bands, and orchestras where one would expect to see the musicians sitting down, reading music and following a conductor's direction, as this is how they traditionally perform. But if someone is attending a dance band performance, they generally expect the musicians to act like they're into it.

I always strive to give myself enough time to memorize or, at the least, learn the tunes enough to make eye contact with others. When you know the music inside and out, the unprepared musicians will naturally follow you to get themselves through the song. The fact that you have the tunes down sends the message to the other members of the band that they need to step it up. Plus, if you're asked to cover a gig without a rehearsal, nailing the songs on the spot sends the message to the other players that you're reliable, professional, and can be trusted.

Playing confidently doesn't come by winging it. It takes preparation and getting comfortable with the music you're about to put out. If you can do this, it's highly likely that bands will call you again and recommend you to sub in other bands.

Tune Up

How do you currently plan for gigs? What are some ways in which you could improve your planning, even before practicing?

CHAPTER 7

PRACTICE

When I ask people how musicians can improve confidence in their playing, almost everyone's first response is "practice." The need to practice may sound obvious, but I'm always amazed by the number of people who show up to rehearsals and gigs without taking this crucial step. Choosing not to practice stems from many root causes. Whatever the cause, it's a self-absorbed choice in which the audience, fellow bandmates, and the music suffer because of it. You may think that the need to not practice is a beginner musician's attitude. But sadly, it isn't. I witness this among professionals all the time.

I was once hired to play R&B music for a wedding reception. All the musicians were professionals and used to playing this type of freelance gig. Several months in advance, the list of tunes was sent out to everyone. As soon as I received the list, I went right to work learning all 30 tunes. The leader scheduled a single rehearsal a couple of days before the wedding. It's common for musicians of this caliber to need only one rehearsal to run through the tunes.

However, much to my surprise, once we arrived at rehearsal, no one knew the tunes. So, the band had to resort to playing standard jazz tunes because that was all we could manage to pull off. The problem was that wasn't what we were hired to play and, as a result, nobody danced. We would've been in a much better spot had each member held themselves accountable for learning the tunes.

Playing an instrument isn't a race. The more you try to rush to the end goal, the more likely you will incorporate bad habits that become difficult to reverse. Success is gradual, little by little increasing in progression. Effective practicing is necessary to have a successful gig, and it also takes deliberate actions to improve your playing. Here are some practice tips I use and recommend.

Listen

Sometimes, I can play a song by simply listening to it once, without even picking up my instrument. Our ears are powerful. The more we listen to and play scales over and over again, the more we get used to how they sound, and it becomes easier to recognize the intervals between notes. Recognizing the intervals makes it easier to tell if a song or a chord is in a major or minor key and which type of major or minor scale that is being used. This can get pretty complex as there are many different types of major, minor, altered scales, and chords. But getting used to hearing the basic major and minor chords is a big step forward if you are just starting out.

As you continue to listen, those sounds become instilled in you and you automatically recognize them. Once you have those down, take it to the next level by learning the different types of scales and chords. Eventually, when listening to the radio, you can hear which scales are being borrowed to make up that song. Having this skill speeds up the time it takes you to learn how to play songs. If you're just starting out playing music and are trying to learn scales and chords, this order is a good progression for your learning.

If the music you're playing already has a recording, get a copy and listen to it over and over again until it gets stuck in your head. This is one way to get to know the structure, feel, and other details. Also, listen for how complex the song is. The more complex it is, the more you'll want to loop and listen to it. You can gain this level of details without even touching your instrument. Using this technique makes it much easier to know where you are in the song and not get lost when you do go to play it. This also gives you a basis of where to start from before trying to make the song your own and putting your own spin on it.

Play Along

Playing along with the music is a very effective way of learning and improving. It's also an alternative way for you to get playing experience when you don't have the opportunity to play with other people in person. You gain a lot if you play along to music that's more advanced than your skill level. Thanks to modern technology, there are several apps that allow you to slow down songs and adjust the tempo to your learning speed while maintaining the same key. They can also allow you to break the song into sections and loop them. This is perfect when learning complex lines and solos. Loops are also great for working on your own creative solos.

Slow Down

Have you ever played a passage so fast that you stopped in the middle because your fingers and limbs couldn't catch up? Or you played the entire passage but missed some notes? It means that you were playing too fast. This isn't how you want to practice learning tunes. You will never memorize music this way because you're not giving your muscle memory time to react. Typically, as soon as people play a difficult section correctly one time, they move on to the next section. If they play it incorrectly but keep going anyway, their muscle memory will get confused and will not be able to recall the previous section. So, when they go to play the first part again, they mess it up, and it's like they're learning it for the first time.

Playing too fast is a bad habit that carries over into other areas of playing and prevents you from getting better. I've played with musicians who learn songs this way. The irony is that slowing down is actually the fastest way to learn. But many people are too impatient to reap the fruits of their natural progression. My advice for playing musical passages flawlessly, and at greater speeds, is to break the songs into parts. Slow down one part at a time and repeat it over and over again. Once you're nailing it every time, increase the speed by a few clicks and continue to play it repeatedly. Once you're nailing that, increase the tempo again. Repeat this until you can play it up to speed or faster so that you have no problem playing it at the intended speed. Then, move on to the next part.

Because you're absorbing and repeating over and over again, slowing down makes you more aware of any bad habits you've incorporated into your technique. It gives you the chance to reverse those ingrained habits. So, when you play up to speed, your lines sound much smoother transitioning between notes. Like many other skills, you learn them in bits and pieces and are then finally able to put the pieces together.

Flex Your Muscle Memory

Playing an instrument is like learning any new skill. You have to practice and repeat. If you repeat it enough times, you will know the ins and outs and will master that skill. Take driving to and from work every day. The routine typically makes you fall into an unconscious state because you don't have to think about where you're going. You have trained your body what to do. So, it doesn't need as much of the mind to participate.

When it comes to music, I always practice with the goal to commit as much as I can to muscle memory. Muscle memory is the ability to reproduce a particular movement without conscious thought. It kicks in by frequent repetition.

Eventually, my fingers automatically move to the right places on the bass without me thinking about it. Muscle memory is really what you should strive for. But I see many people strive to only memorize songs. Memorizing, which is essentially short-term recall, is okay, but muscle memory stays with you longer.

Repeating scales over and over again also improves our muscle memory. This means that our hands and feet are syncing with your brain. If songs are borrowing from scales, I can hold my hands and fingers on the bass guitar in the same position I play scales to learn a given song. The more you practice this, the more your hands and feet play what they need to without you thinking about it. Certain scale patterns are so ingrained in me that I don't think about where my hands are moving when learning a new song. Because I'm not thinking, I'm not worrying. I'm simply playing. For musicians that don't learn scales, they're missing out on all the beautiful ways in which they can make their playing more musical and speed up their learning process.

When I merely memorize tunes, I eventually forget them, and I have to relearn them when playing them later. Ideally, you want to think long-term. When committing to muscle memory, you should be able to recall those tunes years after having not played them. When you return to them, it doesn't take long to pick up where you left off because your body already knows how to react. Returning to playing music after eight years wasn't a big learning curve for me because I already had much of the information stored in my muscle memory bank. My fingers seemed to remember where to go. As a result, I only spent a few months of working my fingers back up and practicing jazz with other musicians before I felt confident enough to play jazz gigs again.

Improving your muscle memory also increases your repertoire of tunes to be able to recall when needed. This is very useful to freelancers who have to learn a bunch of songs for a gig and get last-minute calls months later to sub with that band again. You may need to play the tunes down once or twice. But you have reduced the amount of learning, practicing, and rehearsal time because the songs are already so ingrained in you. It also makes you more adaptable playing in other bands.

Have a Plan B

If my timeline to learn songs is too short to commit them to muscle memory, I always have a backup plan. My Plan B is to merely memorize the songs. That way, I know them well enough to at least be able to recall them in the short-term without looking at the sheet music and be more in tune with what's going on musically around me. But if my timeline is too short for memorization, I resort to Plan C, which is to write out the tunes. While I'm not intimate with the music, I at least can read it and successfully perform it. Writing out tunes flexes my memory. This is due to having to replay the song several times to get the chords, structure, and hits. I'm inevitably instilling at least parts of the song in my head. I can visualize parts of the song and end up being able to play some parts from memory. However, I still keep the chart in front of me when performing because I don't have the complete tune memorized.

As a last resort to limited time, my final backup plan is to merely sight-read the music. So, as soon as I get the list of songs, I search out sources to gather charts that are already written by someone else. That saves me the time of having to write it, and all I have to do is read the chart. But it also means I'm less likely to retain the information because I'm not doing much to reinforce my learning and connect with the song. I study the sheet music and play it. I then compare it with how it's played by the original artists to avoid getting lost in the form, playing incorrect notes or rhythms. If I'm reading someone's original piece and it doesn't have a recording, then I study the sheet music, practice playing to it, and trust that I will pull it off successfully.

Committing your part to muscle memory, or even short-term memory only, will help you remain confident that you're solid with your part. It also frees you up to put your own spin on the music. But the intent isn't to make yourself crazy with trying to memorize a bunch of stuff. The main thing is to be prepared and confident enough to successfully execute your performance, whether you have it memorized or written out. That's why you should always have a backup plan.

Play with Others

Playing by yourself and with a band can often yield different results. For example, you can easily be thrown off by a piano player who may interpret chords differently than you. Self-doubt kicks in because you think you're either lost in the song or are playing a wrong note, when all the pianist may be doing is playing a substitution chord. I can tell right away when I play with musicians who mostly play by themselves, whether in practice or performance. They exhibit a self-absorbed style of playing and don't really connect with the other players when put in a band setting. They usually follow their own tempo that drastically speeds up or drags behind. They tend to add and drop beats in measures. They also tend to be insecure when playing with others.

Woodshedding (practicing) is a fundamental requirement to learning and improving your craft. But applying your skills by playing with other musicians is just as important. It's like conversing with other people. You get different ideas and perspectives that spark more ideas in you. The more you do it, the more comfortable you get. Playing with people will give you experiences that get you out of your shell and take your skills to another level. The more people you play with, and the better the players you're playing with, the more it will force you to step up your skills. It involves facing your fears of being judged, rejected, failure, etc. This is what makes you a stronger and more confident player, whether playing with others or by yourself.

Take Breaks

Taking breaks from practicing is just as important to practicing as playing the instrument. Your muscles need to relax and let the memory aspect of learning catch up. I usually play non-stop in chunks of about 10 to 15 minutes and then, take a break. My breaks are usually about five minutes. This allows me to absorb what I learn and relax my body again before I go back in for another non-stop 10 to 15-minute period.

Your non-stop session doesn't need to be the same length as mine. The important take away here is to ensure that you're taking breaks, however long they may be. There is only so much information the mind can absorb at one time. Playing non-stop for too long will stagnate your progression, leaving you tense and frustrated. So, take a minute or two to grab water and stretch. Whatever you do, try to refrain from doing stuff that can easily get you sidetracked. You don't want to look up and realized an hour has passed before you get back to practicing.

Tune Up

What is your core method for learning music? How do you approach practicing? Which of the methods mentioned in this chapter could you start to incorporate?

CHAPTER 8

GROW, DON'T PLATEAU

Once we've increased confidence in our playing, we need to continue building it. This is done through continuous learning, challenging ourselves, and expanding our possibilities through improving our skills so that we create more opportunities for ourselves. When we stop doing this, we plateau.

When we plateau, our growth stagnates, and there's a drastic decline in progress or none at all. Following the same old routine is a big contributor to plateauing. Playing the same songs night after night, week after week, or even year after year gets old. Having a steady place to play is great because it provides steady work for us. But oftentimes, the same locations will draw in the same audiences, leading to burnout because we're always playing in the same setting with the same scenery. If we're not changing out our list of songs enough, not only will we get burned out, but our audience will too. The situation is predictable and lacks excitement to keep us inspired.

Burnout could also resort from having too much on our plates and not having any direction. This can feel overwhelming, leading to some of us not starting at all. Another sign that we're plateauing is when we are on the gig but feel like we would rather be somewhere else or doing something else. Life and other interests get in the way and prevent us from doing things to help us grow in our music. It might become all about the money, and, if we're full-time musicians, money has to be a priority. But if we care more about how much we're getting paid than the performance itself, this might be a sign that we're starting to plateau.

Fear is also a reason many musicians plateau. Whether it's the fear of failure, rejection, humiliation, or some other type of fear, it's keeping our confidence low and causing us to miss chances that would help us grow. The good news is that you still hold the power to turn this around. You simply need to get in the driver's seat. If you complain because you're frequently playing in these same scenarios, ask yourself what you are doing about it to changes things around. Even if you're slaving away to pay the bills, what are you doing to get the new opportunities that can bring you happiness? If you're not sure where to start, keep reading to get some helpful actions you can take to keep you growing instead of plateauing.

Make Mistakes

When we're confident, we feel free to move and groove through life, unafraid to make mistakes. Even better, learning from someone else's mistakes helps us avoid pitfalls. For example, you don't need to drop a saxophone to know that it will get damaged. However, someone who has dropped her saxophone may have knowledge to offer you. They probably know what the most expensive part of the horn to repair is, how much it costs, and how long it takes to repair. At the same time, you're not going to gain this firsthand knowledge unless you go through the experience yourself. I'm not suggesting you go through every pitfall just so you can gain experience. That would be crazy. But don't be afraid to act and continue to move forward in the face of risks, while also learning from others' experiences along the way.

One of the best ways to improve on our instruments is through trial and error. Like language, music is based on fundamental rules. Once we understand the rules, we can break them to diverge onto a creative path and find our voice. Breaking the rules is how new genres of music are created. Artists who've pioneered different genres were not checking the rulebook to see if it was okay to play what they felt.

Bebop jazz broke the rule of only playing notes that fit into the key of the song. This style of music uses external-key notes and scales to create tension and release in songs. Bebop has opened up a new dimension of possibilities in playing jazz. Much of modern-day jazz has this sound. I encourage you to listen to music and songs that break the rules so that you can explore new possibilities. Learn to play the songs and study how the external-key notes are being applied. Then, experiment with incorporating some of it into your playing.

On my way to every performance, I always ask myself, "What can I do this time to challenge myself and help boost my skills to the next level?" It could be as simple as incorporating a new lick that I've been practicing, altering some notes, singing along, playing the song using a different hand position, or something else that challenges me and keeps me on my toes. I recommend taking such risks as they can do wonders for improving your skills and confidence. But you also have to be okay with yourself when you make mistakes along the way. Setting challenges is a great way to take on risk and make the process of "messing up" way more fun. Instead of fearing failure, you're focused on conquering the challenge you set for yourself.

Change It Up

Avoiding a plateau is all about continuing to grow as a musician. There inevitably comes a time when you hit a motivational wall. You get burned out and lose the excitement for what you're doing. The root causes are numerous and can be frustrating when you're trying to move forward. The good news is that it's mostly temporary and you can manage it. So, don't beat yourself up. This is a natural part of the process and only a signal letting you know you need something new—to change it up. You can help yourself feel re-inspired by engaging in things that motivate you.

The methods for changing it up are endless, depending on how creative you want to be. For me, listening to other musicians play can help me get re-inspired. Something about hearing them gives me the itch to want to play again. But there are days when I pick up the bass and then, put it right back down because I'm simply not feeling it. If I don't have an immediate gig to prep for, I might take a break from music altogether and focus on other areas of life. This is another way to "change it up." Taking a break gives me a fresher perspective when I go back to music.

I also like listening to stories of people who overcame struggles and became successful. That always motives me to work harder, even when I'm not burned out. Continuous learning, setting goals, and having a practice plan are other tools that help prevent plateauing. You should strive to gain as much exposure to different facets of music as possible, to help prevent getting stuck in one area of playing. Collaborating with others is also a great way to learn and gain different perspectives, leading to further growth.

Choose Your Gigs Wisely

This is one of the most important pieces of advice I have for musicians who want to avoid getting burned out and plateauing. For most of us, we simply want a steady gig to help us pay the bills and still love what we do. This is challenging for full-time musicians who sometimes have to play gigs they don't want to play only to get the money. Even if it is not all about the money, we sometimes have to play tunes we are not excited about. But no matter what the situation is, it's important to find ways to keep our overall passion for the music alive so that we can continue to grow.

Maybe you have a standing gig where you have to play the same songs over and over. Not only are you getting bored, but so is your audience. It's time to refresh your set list. If this situation doesn't allow you to do that, find creative ways to keep it interesting for yourself. For example, I may change up the feel of the song a bit, or I'll incorporate lines and riffs that I've been practicing or have come up with on the spot. If none of this is working and I'm no longer excited about the music anymore, then it's time for me to move on and find a new musical venture. Staying in a stagnate and boring environment only creates resentment. I'm not helping anyone if I'm only bringing negative energy to the music.

Instead of feeling stuck, take the necessary steps to remove yourself from the project. Up your networking game and seek out other opportunities. To avoid burning any bridges, you should communicate with the other band members as soon as possible so that they can process that change is coming. Fulfill your remaining commitments, unless you have amicably negotiated out of them, and begin looking for your replacement.

Generally, people will understand, but not always. In either case, try to do all you can to make sure you leave on good terms. Be professional. But also make sure you're taking care of yourself. For the people that don't understand, remember that their negative responses are not about you. They may have simply grown comfortable with you being there and aren't ready to accept the change.

If you have the ability to take on more than one project at a time, try to mix them up so that the experiences between the two are different enough to keep them interesting and challenging for you. For example, I'm in several Top 40 bands. But the category of Top 40 is very broad. Each band I play in is unique, with different sets of musicians bringing something different to the table. One band focuses on more 1960-1990s rock music while another band focuses on more millennial R&B. Even in my jazz bands, one focuses on playing bebop while another focuses on smooth jazz. So, not only am I getting exposure to different styles of music and musicians, but I'm also experiencing different audiences and venues. It's all about wisely choosing gigs that are going to keep you challenged and inspired and still earn money.

Taking on every project that comes my way doesn't align with my goals and probably doesn't align with yours either. Ideally, you want to do all you can to ensure that you take on musical ventures that provide a meaningful and enriching experience that is going to boost you musically. One way to do this is by establishing a set of criteria. For myself, I have three main criteria: it must be mutually beneficial, have a good vibe, and align with my core values.

This check and balance system gives me the power to see more clearly as to whether or not I should take on a project. If I'm ever feeling doubt, I refer back to these three criteria to determine what my apprehension is. If it violates one or more of the criteria, then I know with confidence that I shouldn't get into it.

Weigh the Benefits

First and foremost, I must benefit from the project or gig. Before accepting a project, I always think through the sentence: This project is going to help me (blank). Whatever I use to fill in the blank must be an experience that is worth my time and effort. I also want to make sure that it's beneficial for all the parties involved. I don't want to be in a situation in which I'm the only one reaping the benefits for the same reason I don't want to be in a situation where others are benefiting and I'm not. This leads to resentment and negative vibes, sucking the fun out of the situation for everyone else.

For example, I play in a band that did a free gig at the Horseshoe Casino in Baltimore as an audition to get hired regularly. Fortunately, the rest of the band saw the value too and was willing to drive the two hours on a Wednesday night to play a 10:00pm gig for free. We rocked the place and got hired. I've also been the bass player in bands hosting open jazz jams. These gigs always pay very little, usually nothing more than gas money. But I do them because having this steady gig keeps my chops up for the freelance jazz gigs I get called to play. Another benefit is that I get to play with all different kinds of players. This is great for keeping me flexible and adaptable to handle what they throw at me on the spot. I love the challenge.

While money can be a motivator, other benefits need to be in place too. It isn't always about the money alone. If it were, I'd get burned out. That's what happened in my previous life as a full-time performing musician. I was saying yes to every gig so that I could pay my bills. My joy of playing faded to the point that no amount of money was worth playing anymore. I hated it and had to walk away. I ended up taking non-musical jobs to make ends meet. It took me eight years to come full-circle and get back into loving music again. My reasons for playing are different now. I'm much more connected to the music and am selective on which gigs and projects I take on. The experiences can be new, rare, challenging, or unexpected, as long as they put me in a better place musically.

Know Your Worth

Playing music is an art and a method of self-expression, but it's also how I make my living. So, the gigs have to not only pay, but they have to pay me what I'm worth. Even for charity events, I expect to get paid or compensated for what I'm worth. On rare occasions will I do a music project for less pay than I'm worth, or for free. It has to be a situation in which it will pay great dividends in other ways, such as leading to greater forward-moving opportunities.

It's very important to understand your worth. Otherwise, you can easily get sucked into accepting whatever pay you're offered. If you know your worth, you have a leg to stand on when requesting your expected compensation. How do you figure out your minimal compensation threshold? Research and ask other musicians how much certain types of venues pay. For example, $50 for a 3-hour gig may be acceptable to a beginner musician or someone who is trying to promote their original material. The higher-caliber musicians may require more. But this is only one example. There are many factors involved here that you need to consider, including how many people show up, how well it's marketed, the venue's budget, the number of musicians in the band, and more.

Find (and Give) Positive Energy

Have you ever played in a situation where it felt as if there was a gray cloud in the air? You can feel the negative energy, which can happen for many different reasons. It may be people with ego trips, creative differences, controllers, pessimism, differences of opinion, judgmental behavior, or something else. Whatever the reason may be, it sucks the fun out of playing. But be aware; you may actually be causing it, so make sure you check yourself.

I like to be in settings where there are good vibes with an exchange of positive energy. While I'm serious about the music, I can be a bit of a goofball. I always do my part to keep the situation light-hearted with a little humor and encouragement. This helps people feel comfortable to open up and be themselves, which is what you want when you're playing. You want people to feel relaxed and be fully present. It's then that you can see them for who they are and what they can bring to the table. This is how we learn from each other.

I make sure I carry this positive energy to all my music settings, because we are there to have fun and speak to each other through music. Our good vibe inevitably spills over into the audience. Suddenly, you have an audience that is bobbing their heads, clapping for you, tipping you, complimenting you, and telling the owner to hire you back. See how that works? Everyone is happy. It's possible to please all sides.

Keep Your Core Values

I once entered into a project that seemed promising. A vocalist mentioned that she had studio recordings of her original R&B songs and was working to put a show together. She asked me to play bass and would pay me for rehearsals. She sent me a tape, and I immediately loved the music. When I showed up to the rehearsal space, I was greeted by the lead vocalist and a group of people joking around and laughing. It turned out that the other folks were the background singers and they all knew each other. A drummer also showed up who was new, like me. We all set up our equipment to play.

The lead vocalist had me and the drummer play the songs and loop them over and over again so that the background singers could get their parts together. But the singers seemed to be taking a long time to get their parts right. It became apparent that they hadn't learned the songs. So, the drummer and I were looping one song for a while, basically acting as the recording they should have listened to prior to coming to rehearsal.

All they had to do was sing along with the recording or use a looping machine and then, bring in the rest of the band when they were ready. Then, we would have been a lot further along. But the deal breaker for me was that all the singers were frequently disappearing to smoke pot, while the leader told us to keep the loop going. This was not the promising project I initially thought it to be. It was a drug hang out, and I was being used to provide the live music loop. I felt devalued, while the other people were having fun.

I became increasingly impatient with the lack of rehearsal structure, the goofing off, and the boring looping over and over again. After a couple of hours of this, I decided to stop playing and packed up my equipment to leave. The drummer, also annoyed, followed suit. The leader was confused as to why we were leaving. As she walked me to my car, I let her know that this wasn't the project for me.

While I like to have fun, I value music too much to waste my time with people who don't share my same core principles of preparation, rehearsal, and focus. Even though I was getting paid and needed the money, my higher needs for growth, challenge, and forward movement toward more positive opportunities were compromised. Nowadays, I won't get involved in musical projects that compromise my core values or my relationships with family and friends. It's a judgment call that every musician has to make sometimes.

Be Persistent

It was an early Monday in May 1994 when my dad and I hopped in the car, with bass in hand, for a four-hour drive across Louisiana. I was nervous, and my mind was racing. We were on our way to my audition to play in the Navy Band. My only job would be to play music all day, every day. I wouldn't have to worry about money, a place to sleep, or where my next meal would come from. I was beyond excited. All my life, I wanted to be a rock star. I didn't have a clue how to get there, but I knew that getting to play with the Navy Band was going to get me one step closer.

I arrived at the audition and thought it went really well. Afterward, the judging panel told me they'd contact me soon with their decision. I received the letter a few days later. "We regret to inform you that you did not pass the audition." I was crushed. My dream was destroyed. I kept reading the letter over and over again to make sure I didn't misread it. Eventually, I read past the rejection and noticed that it said I could re-audition in one year. So, there was still hope, but what would I do in the meantime?

I'd just graduated high school and didn't have a job. I had no intentions of going to college, mainly because I didn't think I was smart enough. So, ultimately, I decided to enlist in the Navy and worked a different job until the opportunity came for me to re-audition. I showed up at the Navy recruiting station and took the Armed Services Vocational Aptitude Battery (ASVAB)—an entrance test the military uses to determine what job to place you in. The higher the score, the more job options you have to pick from.

I always hated these kinds of tests because I never do well on them. So, when I took the ASVAB, you guessed it, I scored very low. In fact, the recruiter told me that my score was below the scoring threshold to be accepted into the Navy. But they saw that I really wanted to enlist and they needed to meet their quota. So, I was brought on as a deck seaman. I didn't know what that was, and I really didn't care. I was excited to have a job and felt that I was one step closer to landing a spot with the Navy Band.

My first duty station was a ship, the USS Puget Sound, in Norfolk, Virginia. I sacrificed bringing a bunch of my personal belongings so that I could bring my bass guitar with me. I had no idea where I was going to put it or if I was even allowed to keep it on the ship with such tight quarters. But I needed to practice, so I took a chance. As fate would have it, a fellow shipmate who played guitar told me that he stored his instrument in the ship's chapel. Problem solved!

So, it turned out that a deck seaman is one of the lowest positions you can get in the Navy. Because my ship spent most of the time in port, my job was to paint the outside of the ship all day every day. It didn't matter if the temperatures rose above 100 degrees or if it dipped below freezing, at which point the paint won't stick. It sucked. During my free time, I'd slip down to the chapel to practice. This went on for a year, until the opportunity to re-audition presented itself.

The audition the second time around was an easier experience because I knew what to expect and had been strengthening my weak spots. I played well, and the panel informally notified me on the spot that I passed. Yes! Now, I could finally start realizing my dream. I was on cloud nine, until they gave me the bad news that they couldn't bring me on because all the bass player job positions were filled. I was crushed. Again. But I persisted.

I explained my situation to my ship's commanding officer (head boss) to see if there was anything he could do. He ended up making a personal call to the Naval School of Music, and they agreed to bring me aboard. That was the beginning of my professional music career.

A major part of avoiding plateaus is being persistent. Unfortunately, many people will give up once they feel any doubt in their ability. But there is something to be gained in every challenge. It's through those experiences that we find the toughness and flexibility to persevere. That's how the great players become great. They're persistent and don't give up when faced with challenges. They get creative and find ways around them.

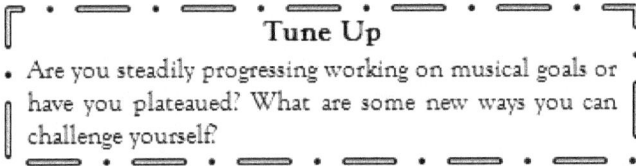

Tune Up

- Are you steadily progressing working on musical goals or have you plateaued? What are some new ways you can challenge yourself?

CHAPTER 9

IMPROVE PHYSIOLOGY

By now, you know that improving your playing confidence is much more than simply practicing your instrument. Much of it has to do with improving your state of mind. And there is an inherent connection between the mind and the body. The body is, obviously, your physical form—your muscles, heart, lungs, kidneys, etc. And your mind operates as the organizer to keep all your body parts working together. They're all connected and co-dependent.

Have you ever wondered why your muscles tense up when you feel threatened, or your palms sweat when you're nervous? These receptions and transmissions of signals are proof of our physiology at work. Because our minds can directly affect our bodies, we have some control over this process and can change what's going on in our bodies. We can also use our bodies to influence our minds as well as other people's minds.

To strive for our best musical selves, we need to tap into our physiology and understand how it impacts our mind, our confidence, and our playing. Performing can wear you out. You need a lot of energy to endure a three-hour or longer gig. The better care you take of yourself, the more stamina you will have for these gigs. That's why it's vital to watch your food and alcohol consumption, to exercise, and to get sufficient rest.

Food and Alcohol

I don't recommend performing on an empty stomach, as it can adversely affect the amount of energy you need to play your best. As for me, I get grouchy when I have to play on an empty stomach. The lack of energy makes it difficult to focus on the music. So, I always make sure to eat something on the lighter side, just enough for me to be satisfied. I avoid overeating because doing so makes me uncomfortable when I'm playing.

Sometimes, musicians don't make the best food choices and resort to eating whatever unhealthy foods are available at the performance venue. I've definitely resorted to eating some of the unhealthiest stuff on the menu. But I'm working on getting better by focusing more on consuming foods that give me physical and mental energy, and that helps lead to better performances.

If you're also struggling with this, I recommend paying attention to how you feel after filling up on something unhealthy. Does playing with a burger and fries in your stomach make you feel good? Experiment with healthier options that aren't loaded with meat and carbs and then, see how you feel and play.

As for alcohol, I know many musicians who drink on the gig. Alcohol is tricky and affects everyone differently. I have seen people drink too much, and it affects their playing. They mess up and screw up the music form. Others, including me, have claimed that it makes them play better. I've used alcohol to calm me when I was nervous before a performance. It would loosen me up and numb my performance fears. At first, I thought of it as a tool to boost my energy and loosen me up. But, eventually, I discovered that it was actually wearing me out.

Alcohol will give me a boost of energy, but it's only temporarily. After the initial boost, I end up more tired than when I started out. I discovered that merely drinking water throughout the gig actually works out better for me. My performances have improved, and I have more stamina without alcohol.

I know it's common to drink alcohol on the gig. But, I encourage everyone to try playing without it to see how you do. If you're always drinking because you're nervous, you may have a deeper issue you need to address. Peel back the layer of the onion and figure out what is bothering you and how to manage it in a healthy way. Alcohol will only numb it; it won't fix the underlying issue.

Exercise

Playing an instrument is physically demanding. Miles Davis once said the reason that many musicians did drugs during the earlier years of jazz was that playing wore them out. They were playing longer sets and shows than the typical three to four-hour gigs today. Today's bands generally take 15-minute breaks between sets so that musicians can rest their chops before working them out again. In the early days, venues didn't exactly have the luxury of playing house music between sets like they do today. This meant that the musicians back then had to work harder and play longer with shorter breaks so that people could continue dancing.

Still, years of wielding a bass guitar for hours had taken its toll on my body. From my left trap muscle to the tendons in the back of my hands through my wrist and elbow, parts of my body would hurt long after I finished playing. Sometimes. the pain would subside only to reemerge days later, even when I had not been playing. Even though I'd taken lessons and learned how to reduce tension in my forearms, I was feeling increased tension in other parts of my body. During my eight-year hiatus, I picked up running as a hobby. It was through running that I learned to be more in tune with my body and to be more aware of every little pain that bothered me.

In order for me to increase my mileage and last longer, I had to stretch out my muscles. Through trial and error, I learned that some muscles needed more attention than others. My tightened muscles and shooting pain were signals that I needed to change something. Once I changed, either I'd have a painless run, or another physical ailment would kick in. I learned that I had to make constant adjustments.

Stretching and relaxing my body became the most effective method for me to avoid pain and cramped muscles. I got into the habit of doing this throughout the day to prep for my after-work run. I discovered that I could apply this to playing music, too, and that the pain associated with playing was a signal to me that I was working too hard, not warming up, or needed to change my technique. I began focusing more on stretching, massaging, and relaxing the muscles needed to play the bass guitar.

I also worked on my breathing by slowing it down and taking deeper breaths. While doing this, I focused on relaxing every muscle, head to toe. I started stretching, massaging, and practicing deep breathing so much that I began subconsciously doing them throughout the day. It's now much easier for me to endure longer playing sessions without hurting myself. This has also been a huge confidence builder because as long as I'm taking care of myself, I don't have to worry so much about injuries holding me back. You need to have a plan in place to endure the physical demands of playing music.

Rest

It goes without saying that you can't perform or function at your best without proper sleep. It affects your ability to retain information, think clearly, get motivated, endure performing, and stay mentally alert. A chronic lack of sleep can cause a myriad of health problems, including high blood pressure, heart disease, and diabetes. It can also lead to obesity by increasing your appetite, which leads to overeating.

Even if you exercise and eat healthy, insufficient sleep can slow your health progress. The average adult needs 7-9 hours of sleep every night. Yet many people aren't getting it because they're doing too much in one day or wearing their lack of sleep like a badge of honor. But that kind of lifestyle can quickly lead to burnout and poor health.

Deep sleep actually helps you retain the memory of things you learned the previous day. This is done through the process of consolidation, which essentially stabilizes your memory. So, believe it or not, a good night's sleep is actually going to improve your recall and muscle memory, making it easier to master your instrument and learn new songs. Don't underestimate the power of rest.

Accept Your Body

We constantly strive to reach the ever moving, invisible bar of unrealistic expectation we set for ourselves. Along the way, our minds are constantly influenced by comparing ourselves to more advanced players. Our inner voice tells us that's how we should play and sound. And when we don't, we conclude that we're not good enough. As humans, we are prone to making comparisons. We are psychologically flawed that way.

That's why it's so important to know that it's *impossible* to play and sound exactly like the next person. For instance, Stanley Clarke, one of the world's most celebrated bassists, has been my idol since I was a kid. He's a tall guy. In fact, his fingers are so long that, as a kid, he had to switch from the violin to the upright bass to make it easier for him to get around the instrument. His long fingers give him playing possibilities that I can't get with my short fingers.

On the other hand, Stanley can't play like me. He can't imitate the technique I use to compensate for not having long fingers. But let's say our finger size matched up, and I successfully mastered a sound that closely resembled Stanley's. The whole time I'm learning his style and every little detail of his playing, he is continuing to evolve. I'd have to be in his presence constantly to chase every subtle detail that makes up his unique voice just to keep up. Even if he stopped playing, I will never catch up. There are so many indirect factors involved, such as his genetic make-up and upbringing, that will always keep us separate and distinct.

This may seem like an obvious truth, but the only musician you can be, physically and artistically, is yourself. We don't want to be imposters. Striving to pioneer our own unique path, with our own unique body, creates our own unique sound.

Recognize Your Capacity

Everyone has the capacity threshold for absorbing stress. Let's imagine your capacity as a drinking glass.

Capacity Glass

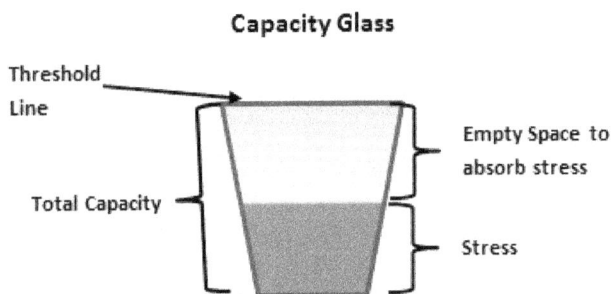

The shaded area is all the things in your life that are taking up space in your glass. This is anything that causes mental pressure or tension - stresses such as paying bills, meeting deadlines, being a caretaker, or anything else that causes you to worry. The clear area represents your available capacity to add more stress. If you barely make enough money to cover your rent, your capacity is going to be consumed with trying to find ways to ensure you cover your rent and still have enough money left over to eat for the rest of the month. If you generate twice as much income as your monthly rent, it's likely to be one less thing you have to worry about, taking up less room in your glass. You have more capacity to take on more and absorb other stresses.

To be clear, some stress can be good—such as winning the lottery, earning a promotion, getting married, and so on. These events can cause stress by taking you out of your normal routine, requiring you to give more of your time and attention to them. However, people generally refer to this as excitement rather than stress because the word stress has a negative stigma. Whatever label you use, even positive life events can eat up your capacity to handle stress.

There's no such thing as a completely empty glass. There is stress everywhere you go. The question is, how much are you letting them absorb your capacity? When the cup is full, you've reached your threshold of being able to absorb stress. You have no more capacity. Taking on more can cause you to get irritable, depressed, anxious, and have a nervous breakdown. Once you recognize that we all have a capacity limit, you can take steps to avoid reaching yours.

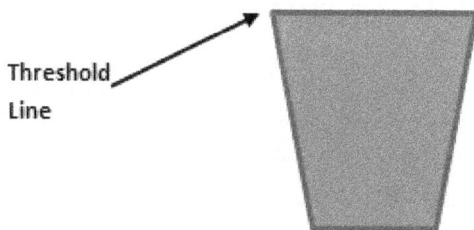

Threshold
Line

Make Stress Smaller

Ideally, we want to keep our known stressors as low as possible so that we have more capacity to deal with unknown stressors that come our way. Many people talk about different ways to manage stress. But I believe the way to get a better handle on it is to think of the bigger picture, which is to manage your capacity level. I think of stress as micro and the capacity as macro. I'm not only managing stress; I'm also looking at my ability to take on more, and making decisions as to whether or not I can. The more available capacity I have, the calmer I can be and the clearer I can see.

One way to get more capacity is to create routines whenever you can. Consistency increases human automation and decreases the need for brain power. If you stress every time you try to leave the house because you have to search for your car keys, establish a routine by always placing them in the same place. For me, the first thing I do when I get home and come through the door is put my keys up on the key rack. Taking care of your future self in this way frees up capacity, leaving you calmer and more prepared to take on new challenges.

This takes practice because you're establishing new habits all the time. Life is constantly coming at you with all kinds of issues to deal with. Some things get removed, no longer taking up capacity. Other things get added and can take up even more capacity. When things are thrown at you, you need to know how to work through the fluff and stay focused only on what is important.

Delegating is another easy way to lessen what is on your plate. You can delegate tasks that are less personally beneficial to yourself—such as picking up the laundry, mowing the lawn, or cooking meals. If your budget allows it or if you can negotiate with your housemates, delegating small tasks is a big way to free up capacity, especially when you have a lot going on.

Psych Yourself Up

A physiological tool if you're feeling anxious or "off" is to psych yourself up. Get your mind away from the cycle of fear by getting in front of your inner critic. Up your positive self-talk by saying out loud to yourself and others, "I'm really excited about playing." Words are very powerful, and hearing yourself say this will manifest itself and become your reality.

Visualize yourself tearing it up on stage, getting a standing ovation, and getting called back to do it again.

A couple of months ago, I went to a job interview. I was a good fit for the position and was prepared for the questions. However, when I pulled into the parking lot, my heart started racing, my hands were shaking, and my mouth went dry. So, I sat in my car for 20 minutes and visualized myself knocking my responses out of the park and landing the job. And what do you know? I got the job!

Breathing is also a good tool. While slower breathing can calm you down and help you see more clearly, faster breathing can increase your alertness and energy. It's up to you to decide what you need. Try to be around other people that are psyched up so that you can feed off their energy. And don't be afraid to stand up to self-doubters by spreading your own excitement on to them.

Influence Others

I often hear musicians complain that the audience wasn't paying attention to the band during the performance. If the audience isn't paying attention, it's likely because of something you're doing (or not doing) to capture their attention. I'd start by taking a look at your visual performance appeal. Videotape your performance and watch it back, paying special attention to the energy you're giving off.

Performing music is similar to giving a public speech. Imagine going to an event where the speaker was sitting down while giving her speech. The audience would lose interest, drift off, and not pay any attention. But if the speaker is standing, walking around, using a dynamic speech pattern, and engaging the audience, she is going to get more people interested in what she is saying. Have you ever found yourself saying something that you were so passionate about that you got up out of your chair to say it? We do this, sometimes subconsciously, when we really want to get our point across.

Musicians do this through their instruments and body language when they're playing. The audience gets into it and reciprocates the energy back to you. That's what you want—a constant exchange of great energy that leads to a good show. Yet it boggles my mind when I see musicians sitting down on a gig while telling the audience to get up and dance. Or even some musicians who do stand but look disinterested; how can they expect the audience to be into it when they're clearly not into it themselves? And if you're not interested, you either need to find a way to get yourself into it or get out of the band.

I am not saying you have to dance and wear a constant smile. But, ideally, you should always bring your good energy to the stage and physically get into the music. Generally, people will mirror you. If you approach them with a smile, they're likely to smile back. Why should the audience act interested if you don't look interested?

I understand that not every type of performance calls for standing, such as big band, concert band, or background music. Also, not all musicians can stand due to the type of instrument they play or if they have some physical ailment. But try to supplement bringing the energy where you can. I play with a drummer who is very effective in bringing the energy to the show. He smiles a lot and somehow manages to dance while playing. It moves the musicians to dance, and we play better. The audience gets into it, sings along, and dances too. In another band, I play with a piano player who has a physical limitation that prevents her from standing. But she supplements by bringing the energy through other body cues and through the music. People feel that, and she always gets a lot of applause when she plays.

I've also witnessed musicians who prefer to look at the other band members rather than face the audience. Face your audience! They took the time and paid the money to see you play, not stare at your ass. The audience is the reason you're getting paid. You owe it to them to bring your best musician and stage self and give them their money's worth. For those reasons, I stand up when I perform. Rarely will you ever see me sit down. I keep my feet and torso facing the audience and give them eye contact while I dance or, at least, move to the beat. I smile at them and I smile at my bandmates. I've even been known to leave the stage and dance with the audience while still playing. I dance around with other musicians on the stage so that we are fueling the energy between us as well. Setting the mood by moving to the beat gives subtle permission for the band and audience to mirror me.

The band's energy rubs off on the audience. If the band is energetic, the audience will pick up on it and feel that energy, sometimes without even knowing it. Suddenly, they start paying attention, bobbing their heads, smiling, and clapping. We feel good, and they feel good. We have effectively created an interactive community. It's dialogue, not monologue.

When everyone is loosened up and listening to each other, a stimulating conversation takes place. Sometimes, I have funny interactions with the other players, such as telling jokes through the music, which is why you sometimes hear musicians laugh when they play. As a light-hearted joker, I'm notorious for this. Sometimes, a bandmate and I are saying something witty; other times, it's deep, with a lot of emotion.

If I can lock in with at least one other player, I can often entice other members to join in the conversation. It's as if we're all hanging around telling jokes or a touching story. That is what it's all about, and it's freakin' fun.

Tune Up

Are there any areas of your physical life (food, alcohol, exercise, rest) that need work? The connection between the mind and body is very powerful, and you can use it to face your fears and positively influence others. Think about how you felt before your last performance. Were you nervous, excited, or calm? If you were nervous, what will you do differently before your next performance?

CHAPTER 10

NOW PLAY CONFIDENTLY

Now, it's all about you. Stop letting fear control your dreams. It's time to peel back the layers to address your inner critic and identify the fears that have been holding you back. The tools in this book are meant to help you on your journey of musical self-discovery.

We are born with confidence. But as we get older, we learn that the world isn't all about us and that we actually have to take responsibility for our actions. As a result, our confidence lessens. Rebuilding confidence begins with the desire to want to get better. That desire can help you break the cycle of fear and change your inner dialogue. Acceptance is a big part of breaking down the impeding barriers. So, accept that you are only human (and so is everyone else).

Confidence is drawn from the willingness to embrace failure, learn from it, and apply lessons learned. It's also drawn from preparedness. Always do your best to be prepared for rehearsals and gigs. You need to play and practice so that you know all of your parts. The best way to do this is to commit as much of the music as possible to muscle memory. Break up the songs into manageable chunks and slow the tempo way down. Doing this will allow you to focus on weak spots and proper playing techniques. Continue repeating the sections over and over again, until you can play the entire song up to tempo. This repetition allows your muscle memory to kick in so that your body knows what do with minimal conscious effort.

The tools in this book will also help you expand your adaptability and be successful when new situations are thrown at you. These situations will give you the experience to overcome challenges, move forward with a good attitude, make adjustments on the spot, cater to the audience, change up the music, fulfill different roles, embrace change, keep a cool head in the face of fear, and push through the anxiety. Seeing the positive in every challenge takes practice because it involves reprogramming your inner dialogue from speaking self-doubt to confidence. Establishing this new way of thinking enables you to rise above the fear. You can absolutely move past it.

Ideally, you want to strive for your best musician self. It's so much more than merely improving the playing of notes on your instrument. It's about having the courage to challenge yourself constantly. It's about accepting your capabilities and limitations right where you are in your current journey while still seeking and expanding your musicianship. It's also about not beating yourself up because you don't know everything or because you don't play or sound like your idols. You're a work in progress, striving to improve.

As long as you're striving, you're growing. So, stay open and take advantage of every forward-moving opportunity as much as you can. If a tool or opportunity isn't working, don't give up the forward motion. Simply look for new chances, and adjust to your situation. Keep pushing yourself to new levels. Planting seeds through these opportunities is to take care of your future self, who will reap the reward someday.

You will see yourself grow tremendously by leaps and bounds.

Use your experiences to help your fellow musicians, and boost them in their journeys. Use your musical influence to foster a positive and comfortable environment for musicians to create and express themselves. Your positive energy and confidence will spread both to other musicians and to the audience. They begin to feel it and feel good. This increases your likability, which leads to more opportunities for yourself. Suddenly, you move to the top of people's list to get called for work, empowering you to be selective of the projects you choose to take on. You become a confidant for people to talk to and a source for others seeking advice.

Applying these confidence techniques stretches beyond the musical application. The concepts also work in other facets of life. They certainly helped me to write this book while managing my non-musical responsibilities. Remember that great musicians are willing to do what the average person won't. You can accomplish far more than you think.

You don't play music because the world needs another musician. You play music because you love it. It resonates with you, and it's a way for you to express yourself. So, be thankful and remain humble. Famed bass player Gary Willis always thanks his bass before he starts playing it. It's a great reminder to be grateful for the opportunity to play, for everything you have in this life, and to share your gratitude with others.

A NOTE FROM THE AUTHOR

I know my life's purpose is much higher than merely playing the bass. I've come to a place where I know how to manage my anxiety and inner critic and feel comfortable with where I am in my journey. Helping musicians to play confidently and to quiet their inner critic is part of my journey.

I never saw myself writing a book. But once I started it, I knew I had to complete it because every day, I hear about musicians struggling with confidence. Plus, I can't think of a better way to reach a wider audience than my own immediate circle of peer musicians and other performing artists.

So, if you're reading this, thank you so much for bringing me on your journey to finding your best musical self. If this book has changed your relationship with music for the better, then my mission is accomplished. I want to hear about your personal journey with music. Feel free to reach out to me and share your experience and challenges. Let's help each other thrive. Now, hold your head up and play with confidence. You've got this.

With love,
CC

ACKNOWLEDGMENTS

When I sat down to write about my life, I didn't expect the process to become a life experience of its own. It has been an outlet for self-expression and a reinforcement of my bigger purpose of helping others. Every day, I am grateful for my family for their profoundly positive impact on my life and their many sacrifices on my behalf.

To my dad, the fighter, Phillip Wilson, Sr.: You forged my personality and shared credit on every goal I achieved. Thank you for teaching me that nothing can stop a determined person. I hope I have made you proud. Rest in peace.

To my mother, Aloha Wilson: I can barely find the words to express all the wisdom, love, and support you've given me. You started this whole thing by buying me my first bass at the age of 12. Your selflessness, patience with me, and encouragement to be better have made me who I am today. For that, I am eternally grateful. Also, thank you for your help and guidance with this book as you read the chapters carefully and patiently and provided invaluable feedback.

To my partner, Andrea Wheeler: You enthusiastically support all of my new projects and are one of the main reasons I wrote this book. Your perseverance and warrior spirit have inspired me in so many ways that gave me the courage to take on such a challenge. The world is lucky to have you. Our story is still unfolding, and I eagerly await the many adventures left to come. I love you always and forever.

To my brother, Phillip Wilson, Jr.: You are the best brother a sister could ask for. You have always made me feel as if you were proud that I was your little sister, and that always made me proud to have you as my brother.

I would like to express my deepest appreciation to my fellow musicians. You bring me joy and experiences that shape my musical career. Thank you for sharing your journey and stories with me.

This book would not be complete without Kiki Ramsey. Thank you so much, Kiki, for being my coach and guiding me through this journey. I am so grateful that you have been in my corner, pushing me and leading by example. You are a true leader who has shown me what it means to not give up.

I would also like to thank my gifted team of collaborators who made the completion of this book possible: Taryn Wieland (editor), Stephen Wilson (proofreader and book layout), Jarmila Gorman (content writer), Sorin Radulescu (book cover designer), and Andrea Wheeler (artwork).

www.ingramcontent.com/pod-product-compliance
Lightning Source LLC
Chambersburg PA
CBHW072101040426
42334CB00041B/1979